"All that is necessary
for the forces of evil
to win in the world
is for enough good men
to do nothing."

\- Edmond Burke

Special acknowledgment to:

Eddie Fennell

For his help and editing assistance.

About the Author:

I was 8 years old in 1960 when I went to the polls with my father in Charleston, S.C. I remember that my farther told the poll clerk that he wanted to *vote* for Nixon as the clerk handed him his paper ballot. The Clerk told my father, I am sorry. We don't have any Republican ballots at this precinct. If you *ever* want to *vote* for a Republican again, you will have to write the National Republican Headquarters and ask them to mail you a Republican ballot. The only ballots the clerk had were Democrat ballots!

Thinking back on that day, that was absurd! The polling place is neutral. The ballot provided by the government is supposed to be nonpartisan! In America, we don't have Republican and Democrat ballots on Election Day. The *voter* gets one ballot with all the candidates on it to choose from. The *voter* can split his or her *vote* between the parties, if they want. We do not have to declare our party or candidate(s) to the clerk. We are supposed to have a secret ballot!

Our state and the nation went to Democrat Kennedy that day.

When I turned old enough to *vote,* I signed up to work in an inner-city precinct on election day, 1973. I was the first Republican clerk in that precinct since Reconstruction (the 1880's). The first lady through the door on election day morning wanted to know if her teenage son and daughter could *vote* using her registration card. Later, a

14-year-old boy came in with a note and his grandfather's registration card. The note said that his grandfather was home on his death bed and he sent his grandson to vote "straight Democrat" before he died. I both cases the precinct chairman and clerks were going to let them vote. I stopped it, and others all day long. At the end of the day, the precinct chairman and Clerks packed up and started leaving the polling place.

"Wait!" I said. "Don't we open up the back of the machines, record the votes and tum the paper work into the County Clerk's Office?"

The precinct chairman told me not to worry. He did the paperwork last night. He got his figures from the quota meeting last week.

Then they all walked out.

I wrote a narrative of what I had seen all day. I reported the end of the day event and turned it into the County Clerk's Office as a sworn statement. I challenged the precinct that day.

The next day the front-page story and the headline in the local newspaper was about Republicans being racist. It was the story about Precinct 7, my precinct. The story said Republicans were challenging the precinct because they did not get any votes in Precinct 7. It failed to report any of the things I reported nor the fact that the precinct had a 150 percent voter turnout and everyone who voted, voted straight Democrat!

There was no hearing or investigation because the Election Commission, made up of 3 Democrats, ruled that my challenge was not valid, because I was partisan.

As I have moved around the nation and attended Republican and Democrat events and conventions, I have always kept an eye and ear open for election stories. I have interviewed the "Pros" of election fraud and manipula-tion. I have worked in elections, managed several campaigns, in several different cities and states. I have run for office as a Republican, a Democrat and as an Independent. I have won a few elections and have lost reelection due to election fraud. I have had my life threatened and have been shot at more than once. I know too much! I have seen too much! I wish to pass on to you the fight-but to win, you must have knowledge. Without it, you cannot expose and defeat what you do not recognize as voter manipulation!

> *"-that this nation, under God, shall have a new birth of freedom ·-- and that government of the people, by the people, for the people, shall not perish from the earth."*

Abraham Lincoln
November 19, 1863

Thank you for caring!

Jerry Fennell

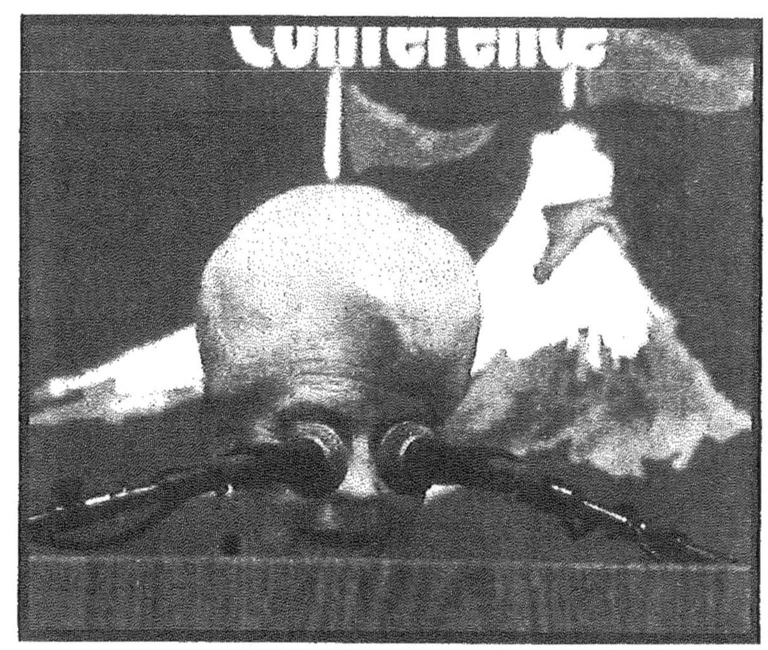

Don't let the messenger
distract **from** the message

Table of Content:

Introduction

The right to vote and the integrity of the ballot are fundamental premises of our democratic system of government. It is the duty of every citizen to see that our election laws are administered in a manner that encourages complete public confidence in the process of nominating and electing candidates for public office. As the technology of voting, going from paper ballots to machines to computer voting, has changed so has the technology of election fraud.

The election process is like spelling. If you don't know how to spell a word, when you see it in print, you won't recognize it as misspelled. If you always see it misspelled, you will think that is correct, right and normal.

This manual is not for those who want to manipulate elections but for those who want to protect the integrity of the ballot and our democratic republic system. If you know what to look fix, you can spot it and stop it!   Every Rule of Manipulation in this manual is based on factual cases of election fraud, theft or manipulation, some published, many never publicly acknowledged, until now.

Is every election manipulated? Is every vote a stolen vote? Can you trust those who run our elections?

The pros don't need to steal every vote, just influence enough to change the outcome in the races that are being targeted and manipulated. It is an art. Less than one vote per precinct made John Kennedy President in 1960. Nixon was elected in 1968 by plurality averaged out to less than three votes per precinct!

If the old election manipulators can register one more dead voter, have a floater voter vote for someone who is not going to vote, switch a vote, discredit a vote or coach someone not to vote, it all adds up!

Our right to vote is a God given responsibility and sacred right. Those who would manipulate this area of our political system are **EVIL.** They are imposing their will over the will of the people. Many of those who are involved in this activity believe that the end justifies the means. Many believe they are doing good.

This book is written from the viewpoint of the Election Manipulator. I want you to think like an election manipulator in order to catch those manipulating our elections. I want you to take this manual and guarantee that your elections are honest, legal and fair!

WARNING:

If you are an election manipulator and you have bought this manual to learn new ways of manipulating elections and defrauding the good people of The United States, think twice! Many have bought this book with the intentions of stopping you!

Up until now, you may have had the advantage! Now, it's even!

Jerry Fennell

Chapter 1:

Meetings

The election process is a series of meetings, If you can control the meetings, you can control issues addressed, who moves up as delegates to the next level, nominations and officers elected, money raised and money spent, actions taken or not taken by the organization and who gets involved.

RULE 1-1:
Control the organization!

Most meetings and conventions are run by Robert's Rules of Order, Newly Revised, Most people are not experts on Parliamentary Procure, Become one and you can take control of any meeting, even away from the Chairman, before anyone knows what is going on!

Using Parliamentary Procure one can delay votes, ram through votes, kill votes, table issue, send issues to committee, filibuster and silence the opposition.

You must be a bully and you must know how to use the Rules of Order to get your way.   The majority be dammed!

Rule 1-2:
Know the value of a vote,

I was the Temporary Chairman at a district convention in Texas, I was holding the election for Permanent

Chairman. I was in the running but had an opponent who was my political arch rival. As Chairman, I knew that the votes each precinct got were based on how many votes the candidate for Governor had gotten in the last election. (I.e.: If a precinct was allotted two votes but only had 5 delegates in attendance, each vote from that precinct was to be counted as 2 votes.)

When the roll was called, I counted all votes as whole votes. One vote equals one vote. My opponent got 5 votes from his supporting precinct but they should have been counted as 10. If it looked like I was going to lose, I would suddenly remember that the votes were fractional votes and do a recount, but I did not have to. I won a close election for Chairman. My opponent never objected.

Rule 1-3:
Get control of the meeting and the agenda.

Once you are in control of the meeting. You control the agenda. If someone comes up with another issue and you don't want that topic discussed, simply rule that you will put that on the agenda for the next meeting. Done!

At the next meeting, simply leave it off the agenda.

You have the gavel, use it! Gavel the person down who is making trouble! Call them "Out of Order!" Even if they are not! If you have to, be a bully!

If they question your ruling, refer to your Parliamentarian, a trusted friend who you labeled an "expert in the Rules of Order." After he rules in your favor, bang the gavel. If the person calls for a vote on his ruling, call him, "Out of Order."

Very few people know Robelt's Rules of Order, Newly Revised. It is unlikely that you will run into one at a local level. Simply exercise your authority as Chairman and gavel them down!

Rule 1-4:
Know who you are delegating power to.

At the local level, most organizations run on volunteers. If you want to kill and issue, delegate to someone you know who will not do anything with it! Appoint a (Black Hole) committee of one to three people to study the issue and to make a report at the next meeting. Make sure they are your people and you can tell them not to do any- thing with it. Now the issue is dead.

As Convention Chairman I had to appoint committees. One was the Resolutions Committee. They were to come up with a list of Resolutions the convention was to vote on. I had 9 seats to fill on the committee. I wanted the committee to support resolutions on issues I supported but I knew that I could not serve on the committee.

I am pro-life. I knew 5 solid pro-life delegates that I had approached to be the committee. To give the appearance of openness, I asked for volunteers to be on the Resolution Committee. Twenty people raised their hands. I appointed my pre-picked five delegates, then I picked three unknowns and the most outspoken abortion rights delegate I knew. (Actually, he had asked me before the convention if he could be on the committee.) I knew he could not sway the five pro-life delegates. The other three, I made new friends and supporters because I appointed them. The pro-abortion rights delegate got his appointment and he was satisfied.

The Resolution Committee repotted to the convention a pro-life resolution by a 7 to 2 vote. The convention went on the pass the resolution.

Rule 1-5:
Make the meeting as long and boring as possible.

Because everyone in attendance is a volunteer and
there by their own choice, make the meeting slow, long and
boring as possible! Don't have an interesting speaker!
Don't serve refreshments until the end of the meeting, if at
all. Only your hard-core people will come back!

Rule 1-6:
**Rooms that look crowded when filled are exciting places
to be.**

If you want the meeting to be boring so people don't
come back, schedule the meeting in a room three times
larger than the crowd expected. Make the sound system
work poorly and irritate the people in the room. If it is
winter, make the room cold. In summer, close the windows,
lose the fans. No circulation makes the time drag!
Find the most uncomfortable chairs you can!
As Chairman, if you can stand on a stage and be
separated from your audience, the more removed you are
from them, the better! Have spot lights pointed at the
audience so they have to shield the light to see you. The
bright lights in the face will make them even more
uncomfortable.

Rule 1-7:
Control who gets notices of meetings.

Controlling who and when members get notices or
reminders of meeting is critical. If you can control who
attends, you have won half the battle. How many "open
meetings" are attended by almost nobody? Wait to the last
minute to notify the people who caused trouble for you last

time. They may not be able to rearrange their schedules to attend. Notify your hard-core supporters early enough for them to attend.

Rule 1-8:
An easily accessible location means people you can't control may come.

Put your meeting in a building or room that is hard to get to and hard to find.

One County Council meeting I attended was in a building where there was no public parking for six blocks! The County Police were outside giving parking tickets and towing away illegally parked cars. At night, it was danger-ous to attend meetings! The surrounding neighborhood looked like Detroit! The public just did not attend!

Council members got Police escorts to their cars.

Rule 1-9:
Be the first to make deals.

I was at a precinct meeting. We were electing delegates to the county convention. We had three seats to fill. There were four people at the meeting; myself; a married couple I did not know and my neighborhood oppo-nent. The couple expressed interest in going to the county convention. I immediately spoke up and said that I would vote for them if they would vote for me.

When the vote was taken, we each got three votes. my opponent only got his own vote. I went to the county convention with the couple.

Rule 1-10:
The Greeter may be doing something "Special."

At one meeting I had invited some special guests to come in hope that they would join and help me gain political control of the organization. They were of a certain ethnic background. I did not know this, but when my friend walked in the door, the greeter had stepped on one of his feet, to stop him. As she shook the hand of my friend, she said, "Welcome to the meeting." Then in a low voice, said, "And don't you ever come back!" Then smiled and released his foot.

The host of the meeting, during his opening remarks, pointed me out and said, "We want to welcome Jeny and his new friends to our organization. We just don't want to welcome too many of them!"

He got a standing ovation and my friends walked out and never came back to a meeting.

Rule 1-11:
Say it is expensive to move up!

If you want to discourage new people from moving up and getting involved, discuss how much time and money (expensive) it is openly. Tell your people privately, don't worry, we can get you a discount or share the cost.

Rule 1-12:
Control the purse!

If you control the treasury, you control the gas the organization has to run on! You must get your person elected Treasurer! If the organization is moving in a direction you don't want it to, simply announce that there is not enough money to fund that activity.

When you have a fund raiser, you report $X was raised, when really $Y was raised, Now, you have a slush fund.

Rule 1-13:
Cleal' the room of media.

You don't have to go into Executive Session to clear the room of media or at least find out if any member of the media is at your meeting. Simply ask, "Are there any members of the media present?" If there are, most simply will raise their hand. Ask them to identify themselves and welcome them. This way you won't be surprised by tomorrow's headlines.

I have found that some of the media will not identify themselves when asked by the Chairman running a meeting. They want to see what will transpire when the people running the meeting think the media is not there. If it is a public meeting, they have that right.

Back in the 1970's a national southern political figure was making a big PR push that he had denounced segregation. A close friend of mine was a reporter for a major newspaper in the South. He was sitting next to me at the speech of this Senator. After the speech, the Senator asked if there were any members of the media. My friend did not raise his hand. The Senator answered the media members questions and then asked them to please leave the room. He wanted to speak to his friends in private. All the media left but my friend.

As soon as he believed the room was clear of the media, the Senator said to the crowd, "I have not given up on segregation! Segregation forever! I just wanted to get reelected!"

My friend's newspaper was the only media the next day to have the real story!

In today's world, anyone with a website, blog or phone is a member of the media. More than one closed meeting has been recorded by a person with a cell phone.

Rule 1-14:
Control the crowd.

To control a crowd, that is to whip the crowd up so the meeting will vote your way takes just a few workers. It is called the diamond system: place people in a diamond formation in the meeting room.

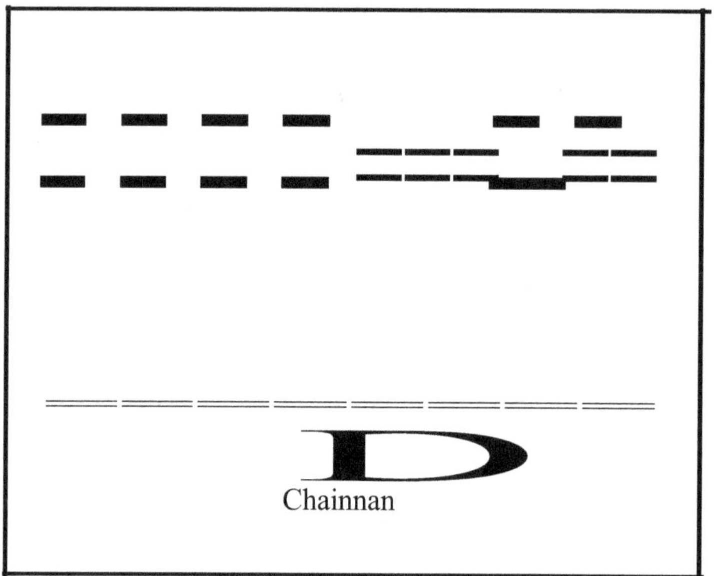

With your people in this formation, you can build the illusion that the whole audience is for your issue! Supporters are popping up all over the meeting room! Whip them up and win the undecided votes.

You can also shout down anyone who opposes you.

Rule 1-15:
Get a meeting room that is **too small for your meeting!**

If you have a controversial issue and you expect a large crowd to turn out for your public meeting, get a room that is too small for the crowd expected. Fill the seats in the room with your supporters early, really early! When your opponent's show up or the curious undecided, all the seats will be taken, filled with your people! The room too crowed. If you can, have the fire marshal or police post someone at the door to tum people away. If they try to come in the room, threaten to have them arrested.

Rule 1-16:
Make sure voice votes are voice votes,

When taking voice votes, make sure that only real voices are heard! I was at a convention for the Teen Age Republicans when I was in high school. We had to have an emergency caucus so we pulled our entire delegation of 125 kids off the convention floor. I was left on the floor with about 6 of my friends tasked with the job of delaying the vote until the caucus was over. As hard as I tried, I was young then and Parliamentary Procedure was new to me, I could not delay the vote. The Convention Chairman called for the vote, a voice vote of about 5,000 teenagers, and to my surprise, we won! We took another vote, and we won **again!**

Excited, I went to my nest of friends sitting in the sea of empty chairs, remember everyone else was still off the floor, to encourage them and thank them for yelling so loudly!

"Keep up the good work!" I told them.

One of the guys moved his leg and showed me one of six 15-inch speakers they had smuggled on the floor under his chair.

Our delegation chairman came back with the delegation after the caucus. To her surprise, I told her she was too late, but we had won both voice votes. I never told her how.

If there is a voice vote that is close, simply bang your gavel and declare the side you are on the winner! move on to something else before someone can object and demand a head count.

If someone demands a "show of hands," have the convention vote on whether they want a vote by show of hands. Make it a voice vote on having a show of hands vote. Here is where being a master of the Rules of Order comes in handy. Have one of your people could do a "Point Of interest," or yell, "Mr. Chairman...." and start talking. By the time you get around to having a voice vote on the show of hands issue, the emotion will be out of the crowd. You have a good chance of winning the voice vote.

If it is close, rule your side won. Bang your gavel. If that person objects to your ruling, call him "Out of Order," and say he is delaying the meeting. Move on!

Rule 1-17:
Make deals.

If you have a large delegation and control many votes, but you don't have enough to win outright, make a deal with another smaller delegation(s). Find out what they want, who they want elected to what office in the organization. Go to them with this offer: "We won't even consider your candidate unless you vote for our candidate (or issue) first!"

Just make sure that your race or issue is voted on before theirs.

Rule 1-18:
Keep an eye on your delegates!

At one convention there was a "unity party" the night before. The convention was to start at 8 a.m. the next morning. The opposition was putting on the party. Their secret agenda was to get all my delegates drunk so they would sleep in the next morning or at least be late to the 8 a.m. morning session. Their plan was to have their people there early, wide eyed and bushy tailed in majority, vote to reverse the order of the agenda. This meant the election of statewide officers would be the first thing in the morning, not the last thing the convention did before adjourning.

I noticed that the bartender was giving my delegates double the amount of Vodka in their drinks and very little in their own delegates drinks. So, I volunteered to serve as barkeep. (I don't drink so I get to hear a lot of stories and can remember them the next day. That's one of my secrets!)

I took an empty bottle of vodka and filled it with water. I used it to pour drinks for my people. I doubled up on the vodka for their delegates! I even stood there, with the head of the opposition looking at me and drank straight out of the water/vodka bottle. Later I acted drunk.

The next morning, we turned the tables on our party host. We had the majority and they were unable to reverse the order of the agenda. Later that afternoon, we won all the statewide races.

Everyone said it was a lousy party!

Rule 1-19
Put a time limit on the meeting.

In the name of having shorter business meetings, put a time limit on the meeting, say 90 minutes. If there is something on the agenda you don't want discussed or something you don't have the votes to stop, bum up the time by talking about something else. (Example; After the Pledge, make a long statement about what the flag means to you. Talk about the meaning of the different colors in the flag, etc.) There won't be enough time to discuss and vote on the issue you did not want discussed and voted on at this meeting.

If the issue is not settled at this meeting, it will have to be dealt with at the next meeting or handled out of the public eye behind closed doors.

> **"Ten men working together· can make a thousand tremble apart."**
> V.I. Lenin

Chapter 2:

Primaries and Nominating Conventions

Primaries are different from General Elections in many ways. In many ways, they are similar. In some states, Primaries are run by the parties and not by the state. In some states, the state runs the Primaries and the state charges the parties to cover the cost of the election.

Rule 2-1:
Control the nominating process and you control the party's nominees.

There are several different ways of getting on the ballot for the General Election. Some parties use the primary system for nominating their candidates. To become a candidate in the primary usually takes a nominating petition of a few thousand signatures of registered voters. There may or may not be a filing fee. If a petition is required you have a chance of disqualifying signatures on the petition, thus disqualifying the candidate. Also, forged signatures have been known to show up on some petitions.

Some parties use the nominating convention. Win a majority of the votes of the delegates at the nominating convention, and you are the party's nominee. Control the nominating process and you control the party's nominee.

I knew one lady that controlled the Republican Party at the county level. She was against anyone new coming to the meetings. She was against a primary for nominating candidates. They use to say that the county party could hold its convention in a phone booth! She liked it that way.

I asked her one day just why she was against grow-ing the party.

She said, "One day America is going to get tired of these Democrats and Liberals and tum to the GOP. On that day, I want to be in control of naming the nominees!"

Rule 2-2:
Find out the qualifications to hold office. Find a way to disqualify your· opponent!

You may be able to disqualify a candidate if you can expose the fact that he does not meet the qualifications. Example: The President of the United States must be native born. The qualifications are listed in the Constitution. President Obama has never shown a valid birth certificate, coupled with stories of his having been born in Kenya. Anyone who can prove that could have him disqualified as President.

Most local offices require the person be a resident of the district they are seeking to represent, a registered voter and maybe something else. There are unwritten qualifications in the minds of the voters: not a felon, good family man, loyal to his wife, honest, etc.

Rule 2-3:
Flood the other party's primary with your Voters.
Nominate the weaker of their candidates!

In the states that run the Primary Elections, in some, the voters have to declare their party when they register to vote. In others, they declare their party at the polls. In other states, the voter does not declare their patty and they get a ballot with both patty candidates listed and they can vote either, but not both patties. This maintains the secret ballot.

If your candidate has the nomination locked up or he has no opponent in his primary, send his supporters to vote in the other pmly's primary.

In some cases, you may have to recruit a member of the other party to run against their incumbent. Even if the challenger does not win the Primary, you would have caused the incumbent to have to spend valuable finances he otherwise would not have had to spend. Also, he has spent months bashing the incumbent, exploring his weakness for the General Election for you.

Rule 2-4:
Who is manning the Polls?

In states where the parties run the Primaries, their own volunteers' man the polls. This opens the door for some problems because the check and balance of having someone from another party is removed. In many cities, city employees' man the polls on election day. These employees could hold allegiance to the administration and party in power. Their job may be on the line if the precinct does not produce the votes the party in power wants.

Getting appointed to work on election day in a precinct is considered an act of political patronage. Use that as a way of rewarding faithful volunteers. Reward them, they owe you!

In the states where the parties run the Primaries, it is the party organization that is counting the ballots. Again, an atmosphere ripe for corruption and favoritism.

Just because the state runs the election does not mean the honesty level is any higher, but it does give the damaged party a better system of appeal.

Rule 2-5:
Control the Credentials Committee. Control who gets seated as delegates!

For manipulating Nominating Conventions just think of them as a large meeting. See Chapter 1. The key to controlling Nominating Conventions is to control the Credentials Committee. The Credentials Committee determines who is qualified to be a delegate at the convention. If you can disqualify delegates, you know are not going to vote your way you can control the outcome of the vote. If you can have "your people" approved by the Credentials Committee, you can increase your voting strength.

Rule 2-6
Swap out the delegates for your alternates when they are not voting.

Candidate Smith's supporters controlled the local County Convention that elected delegates to the State Convention. You were able the get Candidate Jones' sup-porters elected as alternates. The big vote is coming up soon and it is going to be close!

There are rules of procedure as to how alternates replace delegates at such conventions, however, lucky for you, very few people know them well enough to enforce them!

Go to the rookie delegates that are for Candidate Smith and tell them that there are people (off the convention floor) who are alternates and they have driven all the way to the State Convention. They would like a tum at being a delegate for a while. "It's only fair!"

"Would you like to take a break? Walk around? Get something to eat or go to the bathroom? Fine. Come back in half-an-hour: Thank you!"

Then move your pro Candidate Jones' alternates up to be delegates. Be careful that the delegation chairman does not catch you or he may try to stop you.

In just a few minutes, you can change the political mix of the entire delegation. Get enough Smith delegates off the floor for the big vote, and you win!

Rule 2-7
Watch the clock.

I was at a convention that put a time limit on the schedule for nominating candidates to the State Executive Committee. They were only going to allow 3 minutes for nominations. I knew that there were two other delegates who wanted the job. Neither wanted to be nominated first because by the rules, the first nominated would be the last to address the convention. I had a friend with a stop watch sitting next to me.

The Chairman opened the floor for nominations, but no one offered any nominations. I could see that neither of' the men were about to speak. After 2 minutes, I nodded for my friend to stand up and nominate me. He spoke for 2 minutes and when he was done, the Chairman declared the floor closed because the 3-minute window was closed. No other nominations were allowed.

I turned down the position because I knew I was moving out of state the next year.

Rule 2-8
Know your organization's constitution.

One political organization I belonged to was holding its annual convention. A friend of mine held the office of treasurer and was forbidden to run for a third term by the organization's constitution. We wanted to change the constitution but knew we did not have the 3/4 majority vote necessary to make the change. The rule was passed after a person had been in power for many years and turned out to be corrupt. Our treasurer was popular and doing a good job and we wanted him to be able to run for a third term.

We sent about 25 delegates out to borrow every copy of the constitution we could get our hands on. We systematically asked every delegate and officer if we could barrow their copy. Surprisingly we got them all!

Overnight we reprinted the page that had the clause on it that prohibited anyone from running for a third term. We removed the old page from everyone's copy and re-stapled them together. The next day, we returned their copies to them.

We flooded the convention with free copies of "our" constitution, giving every delegate a copy for their very own.

When the issue of running for a third term came up, when everyone looked at their copy of the constitution, it said it was legal.

He won reelection.

Knowing the organization's constitution is as important as knowing Robert's Rules of Order.

Rule2-9
Make deals.

They use to talk about "smoke filled rooms" running the convention and parties. Today they may not be "smoke filled," but behind the scenes, the conventions and parties are being controlled. A convention is like a stage production. Someone writes the script. Someone writes the songs (words). Someone, off stage, is giving direction!

Making deals is natural to politics! Go to your potential opponent and make a deal, if you can. Tell him, you are going to win this election. If he cooperates by (not running against you at the convention or in the primary) you will reward him by introducing his pet bill to the House when you are (re)elected. Maybe, he would settle for a place on your staff as an advisor.

You don't have to take his advice, but it is always good to know the opposition's point of view. Perhaps he will settle for just having close input into the political process.

Rule 2-10
Challenge the entire delegation.

An old trick is to challenge the entire delegation with an opposing delegation. Find some rule they may have violated. Threaten a public fight that will "divide the patty right before the election."

Settle for seating both delegations, but each delegate gets one half vote.

Rule 2-11
Organize an unorganized district and show up with your own delegation.

Find a district, precinct or area that is not organized by your political organization. Example: Smith County. Show up at the convention with a delegation, that you control, from Smith County. If the Credential Committee hesitates at recognizing you, talk about how much work went into organizing the hereto unorganized county. Say how hurt and turned off the people will be if they are not seated at the convention.

You just got some free votes the opposition did not anticipate!

Rule 2-12
Nominating Petitions needs signatures

Nominating Petitions need signatures to meet legal qualifications. If you can't get enough volunteers to pass around petitions you may have to pay them to do the job. There are professional petition companies around. If you still can't get enough signatures, forgery has been used more than once to reach your goal.

"Our best impression of the prince's character and wisdom is formed by looking at the kind of men around him."
Machiavelli

Chapter 3:

Gerrymandering

Rule 3-1:
Know the voting history of the neighborhoods you are joining together when you are drawing district lines.

In the last fifty years, more congressmen die in office than have had defeated for reelection. The districts do not have to look gerrymandered, but build safe districts for your incumbents so they will always get reelected. Gerrymandering can be used to disenfranchise or isolate the other party's voters, religious communities or ethnic groups.

Gerrymandering is the practice of drawing district lines to establish a political advantage. By putting all the voters for party X into one district, you make the surrounding districts safe for party Y. This gives party Y disproportionate power.

If you can control the voters in a district, you can control who wins the election. Controlling local elections, starting at the precinct level, allows you to control who wins local State Seats. The party that controls the State House draws Congressional district lines every ten years based on the most recent Census. With gerrymandering the Congressional Districts and you control who goes to Congress.

Some examples of gerrymandering:

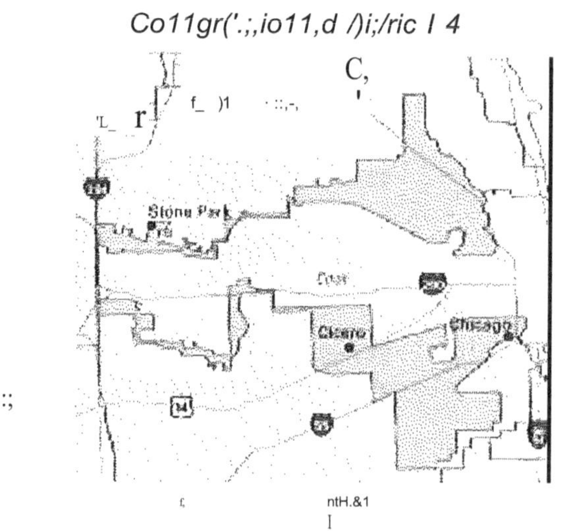

Illinois Congressional District 4

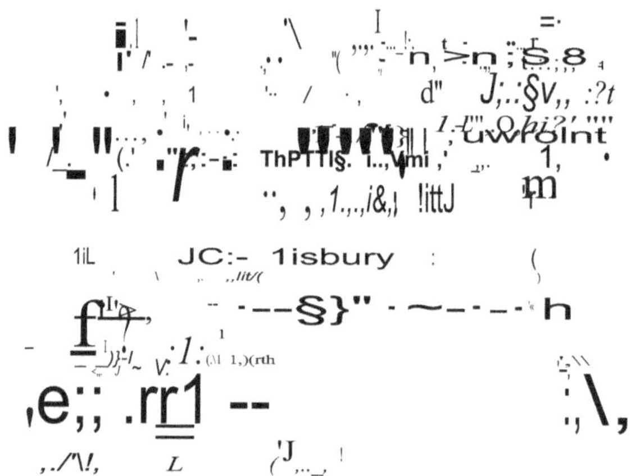

North Carolina Congressional District
12

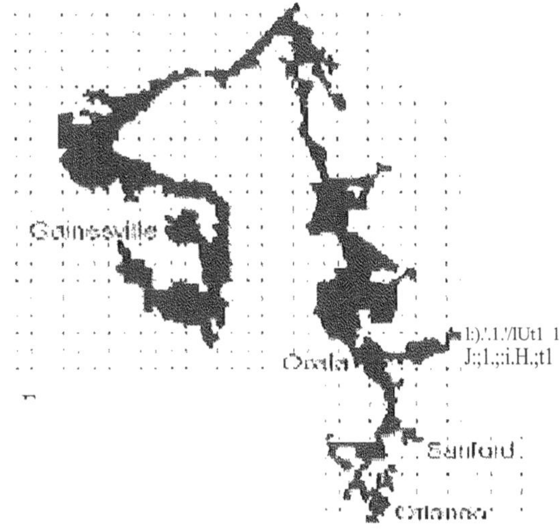

Florida Congressional District 3

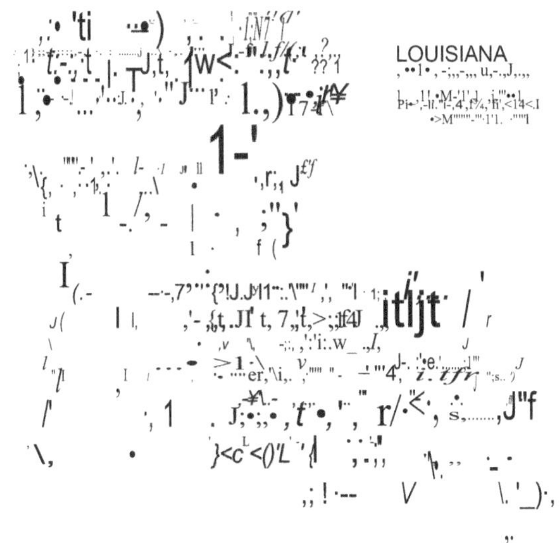

Louisiana Congressional District 4

"Nothing in politics just happens. There is always someone who sets the stage for it, writes the dialogue, rehearses the actors, prompts them from the wings."
Herald Lavine

Chapter 4:

Voter Registration

Rule 4-1

Control who gets registered to vote!

If the Voter Registration Office is in an easily assessable public building with ample parking, anyone can just walk in an get registered to vote. You have no control!

Put the Voter Registration Office in an old government warehouse in the run-down section of town, where the parking is a safely issue, if there is any parking at all. Tow away cars that park around the building.   Have the registration office where street lights are broken and the windows of local buildings in the area are shattered.

If the other party complains, say the office is there to register the under-registered minority community. Say that they are racists for questioning the location of the office.

Don't appoint any Deputy Registrars unless they are from "om" party. Don't have a Voter Registration Van that travels the community to register voters.

If the other party holds a voter registration drive of their own and registers a large number of new voters, find a way of disqualifying either their registers or the voters.

My favorite charge for disqualifying the register is to say that he is partisan and refused lo register nonvoters from our party.

Rule 4-2
Those who can pass as a person on the registration rolls can vote as that person.

Voter registration rolls are public information. Keep the obituary page form the local newspaper each day. Most states ask for name, address, sex, weight, height, and race. Some want the voter's Social Security number or the last four digits, and a signature. Some states don't even ask for that much.

Few have photo ID requirements. Those that do are being challenged in court as causing a hardship on the poor, blacks and women. Depend on our liberal judges to continue to block Photo ID requirements for voters.

Using public information sources, or a partisan friendly clerk in the registrations' office, get this information for each dead voter along with their card number. With the help of a partisan printer, have some blank voter registration cards made. Fill in the information for each dead voter. Find people who match the general description information, sex, race, etc. Assign them several cards to vote for on election day. Collect the cards after election day for use in the next election.

Relatives will often assist in keeping the dead voter on the rolls because it also keeps the Social Security check coming in. If you know someone who recently died, they are still eligible to vote.

Rule 4-3
Register the homeless.

Register the homeless using public buildings as their address, i.e.: the Court House, Police Station, local Fire station. Don't use General Delivery at the Post Office. All they have to do is hang out at the public building for a day

to claim legal residency. On election day, round them up
and give them free cigarettes to vote. We use to give them
bottles of cheap wine, but they could not remember who to
vote for.

Rule 4-4
Register the elderly at the Nursing Homes, Retirement Centers,

Walk through the Nursing Homes and Retirement
Centers and register the elderly. If they say that they are
already registered, tell them that they have to reregister
since they have moved into the Home. Remember to come
back before the election with handfuls of absentee ballots.

Rule 4-5
Register the College Kids.

College kids like to screw the system, especially the
Catholic University kids. They will even vote more than
once, just for the thrill of it!

In one town, the local College Republicans organized
an on-campus voter registration drive. They identified
Republican college students who lived in the college dorms
and needed to be registered to vote. The local Office of
County Elections sent a Registration Van to campus. When
the Republican students showed up to register, the clerk
asked them if they intended to live in the county after
graduation. That was not for two or three years for most of
them. (This is not a requirement or register to vote!) and
then refused to register any student who hesitated or said,
"No," or even, "I don't know. I will make that decision
after I graduate."

She told them to register to vote where their parents
lived.

Small towns that have large student populations fear having the students register to vote, but it is their right. A large student voter turnout could tip the balance of power in a local election.

Rule 4-6
Vote for the movers,

With the help of a local real estate agent, keep a list of voters who have moved away. They are still on the voter's rolls. They are not coming back just to vote. If they are that partisan, they will have reregistered in their new precinct. States are slow to purge the voters list.

Rule: 4-7
Work the airports.

Quietly register people at the local airpot1. People passing through are legally residents, at least for a few minutes. Some airports will allow you to rent a mail box at the airport post office. This gives you an address for the office of registration to mail their cards to.

Rule 4-8
Register Motor Voters.

Take the license plate numbers of out-of-state cars passing through your town. Run the plates through the DMV to get their addresses. Register them in your town using a public building, partisan business address or a Post Office box.

Rule 4-9
Register Illegal Aliens.

In some cities there are hundreds if not thousands of illegal aliens. This is a solid block of voters. The union leaders are best for this work. In exchange for not telling the INS where they live and work, they will register and give their registration cards to the union boss. He will see to it that the cards get used on election day.

I have seen that in states along the US - Mexico border, a bunch of illegals will cross the border looking for work. The union boss will tell them the requirement to work is lo register to vote. They then tum their cards over to the union boss. The workers may come and go across the border, but their registration card slays with the union.

I was told that as much as 25% of the voters in some counties are illegal voters.

Some states require a photo ID to register to vote, but not to vote on election day. This is where states that allow Illegal Aliens (Undocumented Aliens) to gel driver's licenses come into play. Once they have a photo JD, the driver's license, they can register to vote. Once they have that registration card, who knows who is voting for them?

Rule 4-10
New construction, old voters!

Thanks to Urban Renewal I have seen thousands registered across the country! In one city a local newspaper reporter did a review of the voter rolls. (I hate nosey reporters!)

He found that where the new Municipal Coliseum was, all the homes and voters that were there before the Coliseum was built were still on the voter rolls! And the people who use lo live in that tom down neighborhood,

were all active voters. In fact, not a one had missed an
opportunity to vote in the last 15 years!

In another city, a reporter found where streets that
ended in a dead end, whole blocks, for miles, had been made
up addresses and registered votes on the rolls.

Rule 4-11
Police don't always enforce the registration laws.
Fire Fighters don't always put out the flames of illegal
voting.

In more than one city, the local police and fire
fighters registered to vote using the Police Station and Fire
House as their residents in the city. They also registered
where their homes were in the suburbs. I am talking
hundreds of votes cast twice.

City workers whose employment is dependent on
whom is elected locally may be asked to do almost anything
to save or secure their jobs.

Rule 4-12
Unions are far ahead of anything we can think of.

One campaign worker told me that his father
worked in the local Navy Yard. When he was a boy, his
father told him that in every pay envelope just before an
election, he would get a note from his union rep, saying that
if a single Republican was elected in the county on Tuesday,
don't bother coming to work on Wednesday. The Navy
Yard would be closed!

Rule 4-13
Discredit anyone or any attempt to purge the registra-tion rolls.

Anyone who tries to claim voter fraud exists, com-pare them to people who believe in UFO's! Organize a campaign to write letters to the editor. Call them, "Partisan Nuts!" and "un-American! For questioning the honesty of the ballot!" Try to isolate them. Why do they see voter fraud everywhere? "Where is the proof?!" Charge him with trying to suppress the minority vote! Call him a racist over and over. If you say it enough, people will begin to believe it!

What you don't want is for someone to get a precinct voter list and break it down to a list of streets with registered voters by address. You don't want them going door to door asking to speak to the registered voters there. They may find that several people have been registered using the same address and they don't live there, never did. They may find vacant lots with registered voters listed there. They may find business or public buildings where people have registered to vote.

If someone comes to your house running their own voter registration drive and it is not from "us." Call the police. They will know how to shut him down.

Rule 4-14
Have the taxpayers pay for partisan voter registration drives.

Obamacare is a massive taxpayer paid voter registra-tion drive for the Democrat Patty! Unions and other politically active organizations are getting millions of taxpayer dollars to run "Information Programs" for the party. They are being paid to go door to door to sell Obamacare in the

Black and Hispanic neighborhoods. They are also registering people to vote when they sign up for health insurance.
        Many people did not know that they are being
registered to vote! Who is getting their voter registration
cards and who is going to vote in their name?

**"As long as I count the votes, what are you going
to do about it?"**
William Marcey Tweed

Chapter 5:

Voting by Mail, Early Voting
and Absentee Ballots

Rule 5-1
Vote for those who can't.

Work the Nursing Homes and Retirement Centers. Walk the halls with a handful of absentee ballot requests and early voting forms. "You are here to only help!" Be sure to get everyone in the home, especially the Alzheimer's cases!

Voters that sign an affidavit that they are going to be out of the county on election day can get a ballot up to two weeks early, some areas don't even need a reason to vote early.

Workers for one party have been known to go visit the people who did not vote in the last election, and probably won't vote in this election and have them sign an affidavit. They don't care if someone votes in their name.

In a southern town, one local precinct had more absentee ballots sent in than they had walk in voters on election day.

Rule 5-2
Dead men still **vote.**

You have already registered them, the dead, homeless, vacant lots, etc., make sure they vote.

Rule 5-3
Block the Military from voting.

The military voters in America tend to vote Republican. If you are a Democrat, block their applications for absentee ballots, lose them, delay them, make them late so they can't vote and return them by election day.

In a recent election more than half of the military personal overseas who requested ballots form their local hometown election boards did not receive them, an informal survey of the Department of Defonce reported. Another one-third did not receive their ballots in time to vote and return them before election day.

Rule 5-4
Organize the churches,

With early voting being on a Sunday before the election, after church, have the congregation load onto one of your buses to go to the polls to vote. This is surprisingly easy to organize with minority churches in the inner city and south.

> **"Vote early, vote often,"**
> Political Proverb

Chapter 6:

Inside the poll on election day

Inside the polling place on election day is a different world! The average voter sees the inside of the polls and how elections work only once or twice a year and only for a few minutes. Elections are like a $20 bill. You are familiar with the US 20-dollar bill because you see one or handle one almost every day. If I handed you a purple $20 bill, you would know immediately that it was counterfeit and not to accept it as legal tender. As long as the public and general election workers are, as honest as they may be, as good intended as they may be, generally unfamiliar with what an honest election looks like, we can continue to slip past them dead voters, floater voters, illegal voters and manipulate the numbers at the end of the day.

Let's do a little math; In one county, no precinct can be over 1500 registered voters. There are 92 precincts in this county. If by using the methods in this manual a team of election manipulators can out right steal 10 votes, discourage 10 voters from voting and trick or confuse 10 more voters into voting other than they intended, that is 30 votes added to our column and subtracted from their total. If through other means, we have stopped 10 voters from never registering to vote, thus they never voted, that is 10 votes they never got. That is a grand total of 40 X 92 = 3680 votes county wide. That is 1840 added to us and 1840 taken from them. A total difference of 3680 votes.

How many elections could be changed 3680 votes?

Rule 6-1
The night before could determine who wins on Election Day!

Get into the polling place the night before the election. Set up the machines and tables. Open the back of the machines and add a few votes for your candidates or party. When the other party's workers show up the next morning, tell them you have already set up and everything **is, "OK!"**

If they say that no one is to open the machines without a member of the other party present. Ask them, "Don't you trust me?"

Rule 6-2
Get elected Chairman of the Precinct.

The Precinct Chairman organizes the inside of the poll on election day. He assigns who looks at the voter's registration card, who checks the voter off in the rolls, who hands out ballots or directs voters to the machines or computer. He assigns who accepts the paper ballots from the voters. He dismisses people for lunch, dinner and bathroom breaks. Controlling these positions is like con-trolling the pieces on a chest board.

The Chairman will put "his" people in key positions. He will assign the other party's people to lesser positions and positions where they cannot see what is going on.

Rule 6-3
Train your' people!

If you train your people right, they don't have to know what the law is. They will do what you train them to do. Get your people together about a week before the election. Go over how you want the precinct run on election day and who is going to do what. Then when the other party's people show up on election day morning, you have everything organized. They can only standby and watch. When something is going to happen that you don't want them to see, distract them.

I met a chainman who ran his precinct his way. I was the first Republican clerk in this inner-city precinct since the 1880's! The first voter through the doors that morning wanted to know if her teenage son and daughter could vote using her registration card.

The Democrat Chainman said, "Sure, Miss Liszy. Go ahead and let them vote."

The next voter was a 14-year-old boy who had a note and a voter registration card. The note said that his grandfather was on his death bed and he sent his grandson down to vote straight Democrat before he died.

When I asked him what rules he was going by, he said, "The one's my daddy told me." He had run that precinct for 13 years. His daddy ran it for 27 years before him.

He had never seen an election law book before. The only rule he had was, "If they show up to vote, they vote. No questions asked!"

Nothing looked out of place, because his people were trained that this was normal.

Rule6-4
If you can't control the Chairman, control the List of Registered Voters book.

Get your person in charge of checking off voters as they show their registration card. If you have a Poll Watcher or member of the other party looking over your shoulder, have someone distract them when one of your

"Floater Voters" comes to you.

The fake voter may not have a registration card. Just check off someone you know is a dead voter or someone you know does not vote in every election. If that person does try to vote later in the day, simply say there was a clerical mistake. If you know they are not going to vote our way, challenge them saying they are trying to vote twice and turn them away.

We gain a vote and they lose a vote!

In another state, another precinct my friend ran, the clerk was using the phone book as the list of registered voters. When a voter approached him, he would ask them if they were in the phone book.

"If you are not in the phone book, you are not voting today!" the man told them. "It takes about 18 months to get into the phone book out here. If you are in the phone book, we know you have been around long enough to know how to vote the right way."

When a voter protested, they were given a paper ballot and told they were being placed, "on political probation until they learned how to vote the right way."

Most voters don't know enough to know when they are being manipulated.

Rule 6-5
Spend the morning making friends!

Spend the morning making friends among the other party's Poll Clerks and Poll Watchers. Don't do anything in the morning that will make them specious of you. Win their trust!

Around noon, tell them it is OK if they want to go home or out for lunch. "I will keep an eye on things for an hour or so."

As soon as they walk out of the precinct, the election is over!

In one polling place I controlled, the other party's workers would not leave for lunch. They had checked up on the history of the precinct before election day. I staged a fight between two of my people in the hallway of the school. When they went out of the room to see what all the commotion was about and breakup the fight, we won the precinct.

Rule 6-6
Know the difference between a Poll Clerk and a Poll Watcher:

Both the clerk and watcher represent a political party or candidate, in the case of a primary. However, only the clerk may legally address a voter with a question directly. The watcher has to talk to the Chainman about a concern about a voter, then the Chairman address the voter directly.

This puts the watcher in a distinct disadvantage when a problem a rises. The Chairman can dismiss the issue if he feels it is not valid or simply for partisan reasons can bruch off the watcher.

Some states allow a "standbyer" to help a voter with a question. The hope is that this is a neutral neighbor willing to help explain something to the voter. However, wise organizations have "standbyers" standing by! These are partisan workers who will guide the voter into voting their way!

Rule 6-7
Voters will leave without voting if' they think they will have to stand in line for too long to vote!

In one state, the Federal Judge ruled, in the name of fairness, that all precincts on election day had to have the same number of machines. The controlling party had put more voting machines in precincts they won so their voters would not have to stand in line for so long. This put fewer machines in the precincts the minority party won and their voters had to stand in line for hours to vote, sometimes in bad weather.

After all precincts had equal numbers of machines, the controlling party redrew the precinct lines so their precincts had 500 voters with 6 machines and the minority party's precincts had 5000 voters with 6 machines.

The Judge revisited the ruling and ordered one machine for every "X" number of voters in all precincts. This took the advantage away from the controlling patty.

When you know that your precinct is a key precinct for the opposition party and that they are counting on winning that precinct by a large majority, find a way to stop the voting. (I.e. jam the machines, pull the fire alarm, evacuate the building, etc.)

The controlling party sends election workmen into such precincts to do, "maintenance checks" on the machines or computers around noon. They really aren't there to do maintenance, but gum up the works. The machines break down, jam, soon after they leave. Even if it is one or two machines out of six, this causes long lines. Some voters will not stand in line for two hours in order to vote. They simply will leave and go home.

The heaviest times for voter turnout are the morning rush, lunch rush and the evening rush. If the lines are too long, people will drive by and not vote.

Ruic 6-8
Each precinct should be provided with the basics to
hold an election as long as the precinct votes our way.

The controlling party can make it hard for the
minority party in precincts the minority party wins by
putting the polling place in buildings too small to handle the
crowd or with little parking. By putting them in a building
with few electrical outlets, no heat, no bathrooms and by
providing no chairs or tables to work on, can make it tough
to hold an election in comfort and their party workers will
not want to work on election day again. The minority patty
will not have a pool of election experienced workers who
can spot election manipulation because they themselves are
a victim on election manipulation!

Before cell phones, when the member of the
opposing party had a question about the law or a complaint,
they had to phone in the County Election Office, but they
had to leave the polling room to use the phone in the school
office. This left the ruling party alone with the ballot box
for several minutes.

In one precinct, partisan Firemen would not let the
Republican precinct workers on election day use the fire
house rest rooms. They had to leave the polling place to go
to the bath room. Imagine what went on when the only
representative of the opposing party left.

Rule 6-9
Don't let the opposition party clerks' police the area.

The election polling area is supposed to be neutral,
free from campaigning and campaign material. Don't let the
opposition party clerks and Poll Watchers police the area.
Keep them busy doing something nonproductive so they
can't cause trouble.

Sometimes the morning's newspaper may lay open on the registration table where voters have to sign in. The headline might say something like, "Senator Smith expected to win close race today." Seeing this before they vote, might influence an undecided voter to vote for Smith. People like to vote for a winner.

Having campaign material on the election table is illegal. However, somehow it always seems to get there. It could have been left by a voter who set it down so they could sign the rolls and innocently left it there. Most likely it was left on purpose by a partisan voter or clerk.

Campaigning in the voter line is illegal. Usually there is no campaigning allowed within 100 feet of the building the election is held in. However, someone standing in line could strike up a conversation, rather loudly so others in line can hear, about the pro and cons of voting for Senator Smith. Free Speech!

Leaving campaign material in the voting booth is illegal. The clerks are instructed to check the machines after every voter leaves for left behind material. Train your people not to do this. Your party organization will send people into your precinct to leave material behind after they vote.

The incumbent Congressman came down the voter line in the school hallway shaking hands. When stopped by a clerk from the opposing patty, the Congressman said, "I'm not campaigning, I just saying, 'Hello,' to all my friends."

Rule 6-10
Organize the line.

In most precincts, the voter registration table is broken into A-Land L-Z. This way the clerks can check in two voters at a time and the line move along faster.

In one precinct, a different kind of sign was posted.

It divided the line between Republicans and Democrats. I don't know want the Independents did?

Dear Voters:

Due to the heavy voter
turnout expected today,

We are asking that all
Democrats
Please Vote Tomorrow!
Wednesday, November 6!

Republicans, only, vote today,
Tuesday, November 5, 2002!

Thank you for your cooperation!
Committee for Shorter Voting Lines

Many voters cooperated. When they returned the next day to vote, the polls were closed and the election was over.

Rule 6-11
Organize a ballot snitch program.

When using floater voters, to insure they vote your way, give them an already marked ballot. You can do this only when they election is held on paper ballots. They walk-in the precinct with an already marked ballot. They are given a blank ballot when they register at the table. They go into the voting booth, stand there for a few minutes, then deposit the marked ballot in the box. They bring the blank ballot outside to the person organizing the election fraud program and get their reward for voting.

Rule 6-12
Assist voters in voting.

      The words, "I am illiterate. Will you help me vote?" is often a code word for someone being an illegal voter.

      How many people are really illiterate today? Make sure they get help voting our way!

      Unrequested assistance is a great way to manipulate, confuse or intimidate voters into voting our way. One time I voted in a precinct that had a pretty girl in a cheerleaders like outfit leading male voters by the mm to the voting booth. She said, "Now, don't you forget to vote for Walter!" as she wiggled her man to the booth.

      Walter won.

      I was in another precinct and the floater voters were asking, "Will you show me how to vote?"

      The partisan clerk was showing them her party's Master Lever.

      In a Texas precinct, a man with a rifle sat behind the voting booth and advised people how to vote.

      It is a misnomer that someone sitting behind the booth can tell how a citizen is voting. No one can see how you are voting if the curtain is properly closed.

Rule 6-13
The use of Police and Firemen in the polls.

      Police are not to be in the election polls unless called by a majority of the election managers. They may come to vote, but must leave after voting. The presence of Police may intimidate some people into not showing up at the polls. Police have been used to remove or arrest people who object to election fraud from the precinct.

      In a South Carolina precinct, local police came into the polling place on election day and took the list of people to challenge away from the Republican Poll Watcher. They told him if he challenged anyone else that he would be arrested. The Poll Watcher gave him the list because Police are authority figures and he did not know the law.

It has been known to happen: someone pulls the fire alarm. The building is evacuated. All voters and election officials leave the building. Firemen rush in. After a few minutes, they leave, saying everything is, "all clear." The election resumes.

The firemen had paper ballots stuffed in their fire coats. They stuffed the ballot boxes when everyone was out of the room and then called the building, "clear."

Rule 6-14
The name tags on the face of the machine can be moved.

On some machines the candidates' names are printed on a long strip of paper. All the Democrats on row 1 and the Republicans are on row 2. In a heavily Republican precinct, the strip of names can be reversed. The voter unknowingly will think he is voting for the Republican when he is voting for a Democrat.

Rule 6-15
Don't eat anything unless you brought it.

In one precinct during a hotly fought primary election, one side of divided poll managers staff offered to buy lunch for the other side, as a peace and unity offering. When lunch arrived, both sides ate.

At the end of the day, the side that bought the lunch was well and counting the ballots while the other side was in the bath rooms with great intestinal discomfort.

Rule 6-16
Don't let the opposition wear· intimidating badges.

The Republican Party Poll Watchers have worn badges that state, "Federal Election Observer." Yes, they are observing a Federal Election, if someone is on the ballot for Congressman, Senator or President. However, the word, "Federal" implies that they are something like the FBI or have police powers. This has intimidated floater voters in many precincts.

Object to the use of, "Federal Election Observer" badges on the grounds of voter suppression.

Rule 6-17
When the polls close, make the witnesses leave.

After the polls close, remove the public from the room so there are no witnesses.

When recording the votes from the machines, if the opposition party won the race, simply reverse the totals. Example: 600 people voted all day. Jones got 400 votes and Smith got 200. On the official report, Give Jones 200 votes and Smith 400. The total votes are still 600. If caught, claim clinical error. No wrong doing.

Rule 6-18
Buying Votes,

It used to be that when you voted you were given a receipt, a note saying that you had voted. Union members could take their receipt to a union bar and exchange it for two free drinks.

Now you get an "I voted!" sticker. There are still "rewards" for voting if you know the right bar to go to.

Rule 6-19
Control who challenges illegal voters,

In most states when a person shows up at the polls
and wants to vote, and they have no ID, don't know their
address and has no registration card, they are still allowed to
vote a Challenged Ballot or Provisional Ballot.

The voter is given a paper ballot lo vote on and
returns it to the clerk who puts it in an envelope and seals it.
The words, "CHALLENGED BALLOT," are written on the
envelope along with the name of the voter, the challenging
clerk's name and the reason for the challenge.

Two days after the election, a hearing is held to
review the ballots. The voter is not required to show up,
but the challenging clerk is. If the clerk does not show up
to explain lo the Election Board why the ballot should not
be counted, the envelope is opened and the ballot is
counted.

In special precincts, the floater voter is instructed to
go to one of "our" checks. A code word is used as they
approach the registration table. The floater voter knows he
may be challenged, but if he is, that the clerk will not show
up for the hearing. His illegal vote will be counted.

The clerk can tell the other party's clerks, "We are
really cracking down on election fraud here. We challenged
over X number of voters today!" knowing that every one of
the challenged votes will be counted.

Several close elections have been decided by such
exercises.

Rule 6-20
No ballots are to be counted until the polls dose!

In many precincts around noon, workers show up
and say they are from the court house to pick up the ballot

boxes. They want to begin counting the ballots voted so far
so the count does not go so far into the night. In reality,
they are counting to find out how many votes they need to
steal to win at the end of the day. No ballots are to be
counted or removed from the precinct before the election is
over and the polls closed.

Don't let the opposition pull this on you!

Rule 6-21
**Hold your votes back until you see how many you need
to win the district.**

Ever wonder why places like Detroit and Chicago
are so late in reporting their votes, but other cities seem to
be able to count their votes and report them soon after the
voting polls are closed?

They are holding their votes back to see how many
votes they need to win the election! Once they know, the
election is over. They win!

> **"The seeds of political success are sown far
> in advance of election day,"**
> Theodore Roosevelt

Chapter 7:

Outside the poll on election day

Rule 7-1:
Control the Precinct Polling Place Chairman.

As Precinct Chairman you control what everyone is doing. If a voter comes in and complains that someone is sitting at the door steps of the building handing out campaign material, it is the Chainman who goes to check it out or sends someone to run them off (There is not to be any campaigning with in X number of feet from the polling place.)

A partisan Chainman can go and talk to the campaigner and give him a warning and wink, wink, tell him to leave.

It is the Chainman who decides to call the Police, if they are need.

Rule 7-2:
Control the opposition campaigners.

Use the Police to intimidate or arrest campaigners that are legal, but campaigning at your precinct polling place.

At one precinct, the Police told a campaigner to stand behind a telephone poll that was way out of the zone. At another, cars of the opposition poll workers were towed **away**

Police have been used to intimidate poll watchers as they show up to work on election day, some have been

arrested. Voters wearing campaign buttons trying to enter
the polling location have been turned away by Police. If
they objected, they were arrested and held until the polls
closed, never allowed to vote.

In one election, the Chainman went outside and told
the oppositions campaigner that he had received a phone
call from their party headquarters and that they wanted to
meet them at a local restaurant in half an hour. All the
campaigners left. There was no such phone call, no meeting. It took hours for them to return.

Rule 7-3
Get to the polls early and park your car next to the entrance to the poll.

Get to the poll early and park your car next to the
main door to the poll. Park nose-in and have bumper
stickers on the back of your car promoting your
candidate(s) or patty. If an election worker from the other
party complains, explain that your car is an "official" car and
needs to be parked there. If they continue to complain, tell
them to write a letter to the Election Board.

Rule 7-4
Delivering the votes.

In one county, the County Sheriff was using the prison bus
on election day to drive from precinct to precinct. At each
polling place he would drop off a bus load of floater voters,
wait as they voted and reloaded and drive to the next
precinct polling location. He did this all day long. What he
did not know was that the local TV station camera crew was
following him in an unmarked van and filming him break the
law.

If you try this, make sure you are not followed!

Rule 7-5
Kill your opponent, not for real, on paper!

In one party primary, the challenger had precinct workers had out a flyer as people showed up lo vote saying that the incumbent had suddenly died last night. If the voter voted for the dead candidate and he won, the party would have to hold another primary election. This would cost the party a lot of money that they did not have and could be used to run the fall campaign on.

The incumbent had not died. He could not combat the flyer in time to save his seat.

**"A straw vote only shows which way
the hot air blows."**
OHenry

Chapter 8:

Paper Ballots

Rule 8-1
The paper ballot is the easiest thing the steal.

It's not what goes into the ballot box, it's what comes out that counts!

Boss Tweed (New York City) once said, "I don't care how you vote, as long as I get to count the ballots!"

Rule 8-2
Tell the would-be voters to mark their paper ballot in pencil.

Tell the voters as you hand them a blank paper ballot to be sure to only mark the ballot in pencil, and not to make their mark too heavily. If the mark is too dark, someone may be able to see through the back of the ballot and determine how they voted.

What you are really telling them is, "don't mark the ballot too heavily so later we can erase your light mark and remark the ballot our way."

Rule 8-3
Have your worker put the paper ballots in the ballot box, not the voter.

The election clerk sat next to the ballot box. The voter, after marking his ballot would hand their ballot to the clerk. The clerk would open the folded ballot and take a look at it. If the voter had voted "his way," the clerk would put the ballot in the ballot box. if the voter had voted, "the other way," the clerk would put the ballot in another box.

Rule 8-4
Don't let the opposition check the ballot box before the election begins.

The opposition clerks may want to check the ballot box to make sure it is empty before the polls open. Distract them! Tell them you checked it last night.

Many an election was won before the polls opened by already marked ballots being placed in the ballot box before the polls opened.

Rule 8-5
String Voting.

String voting can be used on paper ballots or machine voting. The voter is given a string with knots in it. When laid out on the ballot or machine face, where the knot is the voter is instructed to vote for that candidate. This is not illegal, unless the voter is being paid with money or liquor or had been intimidated.

Rule 8-6
Don't seal every vote. It won't look good,

It is reported that in Chicago, in more than one precinct, the ballot box staffers put ballots marked for Republicans into the ballot boxes, just so the election will not look so one sided and questions won't be asked.

Rule 8-7
Organize a ballot switch program.

When using floater voters, to insure they vote your way, give them an already marked paper ballot. They walk-in the precinct with an already marked ballot. They are given a blank ballot when they register at the table. They go into the voting booth, stand there for a few minutes, then deposit the marked ballot in the ballot box. They bring the blank ballot outside to the person organizing the election fraud program and get their reward for voting.

Rule 8-8
Create confusion.

When there are a lot of people in the precinct polling place, hand out paper ballots to people before they are checked through by the clerks. This creates confusion as to who should be voting and who should not be voting, yet. Take advantage of this time to deposit marked ballots in the ballot box.

Rule 8-9
Count ballots early.

Start counting paper ballots early in the day. Some start at noon others around 4 p.m. The law is that no ballots can be counted until after the polls close.

If you start counting early, you will know how many votes you have to steal in order to win the election.

Rule 8-10
Counting ballots at the end of the day.

When counting paper ballots, you want to count all your votes and discount your opponent's votes.

In most cases, the ballot box is unlocked and opened. The paper ballots are removed from the ballot box and unfolded and placed in piles for counting.

Create several piles of ballots. One or two piles of ballots marked for your party and another one or two piles marked mostly for the other party, but mix in ballots for your party into the pile. When calling out the votes, you can, with several piles in front of you, recount a stack that is mostly in favor of your party. Recount the stack you created that is "stacked against" your opponent.

When handling the paper ballots, if you are picking up a stack of your opponent's votes, pickup two or three al a time, but only count the top ballot. Then discard the stack in your hand as counted. They just lost two to three votes!

If you are calling out the makings and no one is looking over your shoulder, call out their votes as your votes. At the end of the night, the number should equal the total vote cast. This is a check and balance system used but it does not honestly prove anything.

If the precinct is going against you, make several stacks of ballots. Only count half to two-thirds of them and say that is all. The other party just lost a bunch of votes.

Discrediting a ballot for them is just as good a getting an extra vote for us! Put a small piece of pencil lead under your thumbnail or take a ring and on the bottom side of the ring, drill a small hole. Put a piece of pencil lead in the hole. When you find a ballot marked for the other party mark the ballot showing that the voter voted for two candidates in that race. The ballot is thrown out and not counted.

If you are in total control of the precinct, and there

are no clerks or watchers from the other party there during the voting or counting, just make up the numbers you need.

Did you get your numbers from the Quota Meeting?

If you have a legal eagle watching your every move all day and during the count, have in your car a duplicate set of paperwork. He will watch you put the locked box into your car for transporting downtown after the election. When you get to the County Clerks Election Headquarters, simply pull out the box prepared last night and tum those into the Clerk's Office.

Rule 8-11
You are the Judge as to how the voter voted.

When counting ballots, you have a lot of leeway as to interpreting the intentions of a voter. The ballot below was counted as a "Straight Ticket" for the Democrats. The Democrat U.S. Senator incumbent, whose name was not even marked was given a vote and won reelection by less than 10 votes statewide.

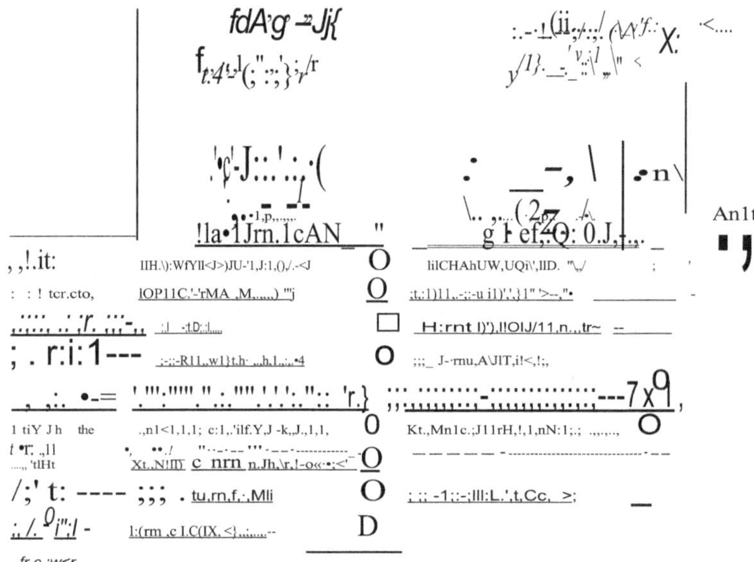

"Go hunting where the ducks are."

Political Proverb

Chapter 9:

Machines

Manufacturers of voting machines claim that their machines are fool proof, rig proof: jam proof, and that it is impossible to overvote or spoil ballots so they won't be counted.

Rule 9-1
Don't let the opposition check the machine before polls open.

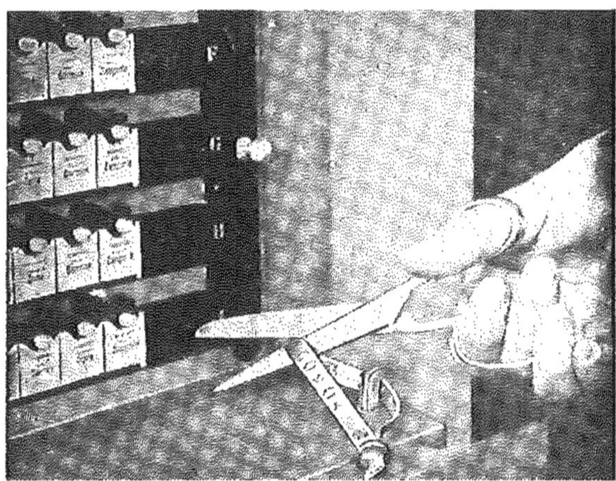

The machines are to be checked and cleared by the election office before being shipped to the polling locations. The machines are to be sealed with a metal seal with a number on it. The seal is cut by the chairman and returned to the election office after the election. If you are going to tamper with the machine, be sure to have your own seal to replace the real one with.

Before the polls open, the poll chainman is to certify that no one has voted on the machines. The counters for all the candidates and the dial showing total votes are to read, "0000." If your machines have been set up to show that your party started with 200 votes, don't let the opposition party's clerks see this. Get to the polls early. When they show up, tell them you have already checked the machines and they are, "OK!"

In one precinct the watchers will swear that no more than fifteen people voted all day, but when the machines were opened and votes record at the end of the day, 98 percent of the people on the registration rolls had voted in alphabetical order (in the same hand writing and same pen) and they all voted for the same party, a straight party ticket.

Rule 9-2
The lever won't count the vote cast if it is **not pushed completely down.**

Since a voting machine's lever must be pushed down completely in order for the vote to count, wedge a match stick, hairpin, razor blade or paper clip under the other party's lever so that the votes for them fail to register. It will be as if the voter never voted for that candidate at all.

Rule 9-3
If **the curtain** is **not closed right, the votes won't count.**

Votes won't he recorded if the voting machine's curtain is not closed tightly. Fix one machine's curtain release cord so that the machine's curtain does not close folly. Steer voters into this machine that you have identified as going to vote against your way.

Rule 9-4
**Switch the names of the candidates on the face of the
voting machine.**

Get to the polls early and before the other party's
election workers arrive', switch the names on the face of the
machine. The labels can be slid over one lever or the who
party list can be reversed, i.e.: The Democrats candidates
are on the top row, the Republicans are on the second row.
Now, the Republicans are on the top row and the Democrats are on the bottom row. This is helpful if you are a
Democrat in a heavily Republican precinct. All the intended
Republican votes turn into Democrat votes.

Do this on all the machines in your precinct so the
opposition does not notice anything out of place.

In one election, the names of the candidates of the dominate party were all printed in bold capital letters. The opposition party's candidates' names were not.

Make sure the other party's clerks don't check the machine after every voter. They will be looking for left behind campaign ligature.

I have seen the levers of the other party's candidate wired so no one could vote for them. On one machine, someone had used Super Glue to glue all the Republican levers so no one could vote for them. Also, in one precinct, if you touched any of the Republican Party's candidates levers you got an electrical shock.

Using the same color tape, you can just cover up a name on the face of the machine. Most voters will not even notice that the name is gone. Until it is caught, that candidate will lose votes.

In one county, the names of the opposition party's candidates from the election two years ago were on the machine, while the party in power candidate's names were current.

I saw where someone had scratched the word, "Right" over the name of one candidate on the machine.

In most cases, I have found that voters will vote for someone else or not vote at all in a race rather than complain or ask for assistance.

Rule 9-5
If the other party's voters turn out heavily, jam a few machines.

When the other party's votes turned out much heavier than expected, the controlling party will have workers come in the polling place claiming to be from election headquarters to check the machines for maintenance.
Shortly after, several of the machines will jam! (8ee Rule 9-

2). Long lines developed. Many of the voters will leave without voting not wanting to stand in line for hours.

With several machines down, in one precinct, the Chairman suddenly found "emergency" paper ballots to hand out. However, a few of the key local races were left off these paper ballots?! (See Chapter 8 on how to handle paper ballots.)

If you know that this precinct is going for the opposition in a big way, don't wait for the polls to open. When you are there early setting up make sure that you do not have enough extension cords to run all the machines. Lose a few! It will take hours to replace them. By then you will have long lines and many of the people will leave without voting.

Rule 9-6
Give the voter instructions and assistance on how to vote.

Improper instructions are a great way to influence and manipulate a voter right before and as they enter the voting machine. I have seen everything from a young girl dressed in a cheerleader like dress taking the arm of the male voter and walking them to the booth. As the men entered the booth, she would say, "Don't forget to vote for Walter!" to election clerks tapping their finger next to the Master Switch on the machine and day, "Don't forget to vote." As if someone walking into a voting machine would forget to vote before leaving.

One man entered the machine and closed the curtain. After a few minutes and the clerk not hearing any clicking coming from behind the curtain, she asked the man if he was done voting.

"They said that you would show me who to vote for." the man replied.

In other election, as the voter showed their registration card and signed in, the clerk would say, "You are voting on a Constitutional Amendment today, and you want to vote **"Yes!""**

Have someone stand behind the machines while people vote. Most voters do not know that someone standing behind the machine cannot tell how they are voting. This will intimidate some into voting for the incumbent.

In the early days of large-scale voting by African Americans, they were told that the "Black candidates were on the top row and the white candidates were on the bottom row." Actuarially, the Democrat candidates were on the top row and the GOP candidates were on the bottom row.

Using the assistance laws, you can offer help to almost any voter. Once behind the curtain, tap or run your finger over the levers you are demonstrating to the voter on how to vote.

Rule 9-7
Full Slate Voting

The U.S. Supreme Court has ruled this unconstitutional but some local governments still use it today and will until someone challenges it. It is called the Full Slate Law.

The Full Slate Law states that if the voter does not vote for a certain number of candidates, then their vote will not be counted. Example: A county has seven representatives in the State House. The Full Slate Law says that a voter must vote for seven candidates or his or her vote will not be counted. If the opposition party only fields five candidates, then a supporter has to vote for at least two members of the other party for their votes to count. The voters are forced to vote for someone they do not support.

The proper law or instructions should be, "Vote for

no more than X." The voter has the right to only vote for one candidate, if that is what he or she wants to do.

I ran for reelection for a seat on a local Water and Sewer Board in Texas. There were three seats open. There were four candidates. This was a nonpartisan election. You did not have Republicans vs. Democrats. The group in power held two of the seats. I held the third. They put up a candidate to run against me.

The instructions on the paper ballot read, "Vote for Three." I objected. The lawyer for the Board told me to, "Go fly a kite."

I called the U.S. Justice Depatlment, Voter Registration Division. The man in Washington, D.C. phoned the Secretary of State of Texas. She sent a certified letter to the lawyer of the Water Board. They reprinted the ballots with the proper instructions and sent me a bill for $1,700 for "printing." (They only printed 800 one-page ballots.) The lawyer threatened to put a lien on my house and then foreclose on me if I did not pay within 10 days.

I wrote back saying that it was the governments job to provide legal ballots. I should not have to pay for the reprinting of illegal ballots. I sent a copy to the U.S. Justice Department contact.

The election was held. The Poll Chairman told me and others as we were given our ballots, to only vote in pencil. (Rule 8-2)

I was told I had lost my bid for reelection by one vote. The counting of the ballots had been moved from the polling place to the home of the Chairman of the Water Board. They took eight hours to count 80 ballots.

At the recount hearing, I found six ballots where the mark next to my name had been erased and remarked for another candidate. The Board voted 4 to 1 (my vote) to certify the election.

My lawyer told me that it would cost $10,000 to

challenge the election in court, but I had a good chance of winning

The State Attorney General said, "There's not enough headline value for me to come an investigate your election."

Rule 9-8
After the polls close,

Everyone wants to get out of there as soon as possible and go to their party's victory party! It's been a long day, sometimes 15 hours long,

After the polls close, clear the room of any witnesses. Tell stander byers that they have to leave. You can try to tell the Poll Watchers, but if they have been properly trained, they will know that they don't have to leave.

A Voting Machine is just like a large adding machine. It just adds up the number of times a lever has been thrown during the day. Open the back of the machine and record the votes. The election workers will be looking at lever numbers. Working fast, the numbers can be deliberately transposed. Thus, 743 votes for candidate A can be called out for candidate B. The total vote will check out correct on the machine.

You can always just add wrong. 200 votes form machine 1, plus 185 votes from machine 2, plus 305 votes from machine 3, equals 790 votes. Congratulations, your candidate just got 100 extra votes.

If the poll watchers and clerks for the other party won't allow you to play with the numbers, have a copy of the paper work in your car already filled out to the numbers you wanted. Have them follow you to your car and witness that you put the locked box in your car. They can even follow you to the Court House to tum in the paper work.

Remove from your car the box of paper work you

want to tum in.

Rule 9-9
Machines are for counting.

In one race the opposition party's candidate won by 57 votes. The County had a recount. They found a voting machine in the County Warehouse that had never been delivered or used on election day. It had 59 votes for the incumbent on it.

The Election Commission Chairman was quoted in the newspaper saying, "machines are for counting."

In the old Soviet Union an old Russian voter, · was standing in line holding a sealed envelope containing his ballot, Curious, he opened it and was chided for doing so.

"But, comrade, I just wanted to see how I was voting."

He was informed brusquely, "You are not allowed to! This is a secret ballot election!

Told by George Abrams of the
Honest Ballot Association

Chapter 10:

Electronic Voting
(Computers Voting)

Rule 10-1
It takes special skills and technological knowledge to rig a computer voter system. If you don't have those skills, hire someone who does.

City, County and State administrations that have computer electronic voting systems have the technical personnel to run them. However, few states require a background check on these people. A layman cannot tell if a computer is programmed to count every tenth vote of the challenger as one for the incumbent or not just by looking at it! There is little or no public information available on the testing of these machines. Programmed by the right person, the counter machine will pass every test thrown at it.

How do you prove, after the fact, that the software in the voting machine is the software that was approved by

the Board of Examiners and tested by the independent
testing authority? Most Election Officials will not have a
computer chip (program) to compare with the one found in
the machine on election day.

If a voter suspects something their only recourse is
to call a phone number at the local Election Board and
lodge a complaint. That complaint may or may not be
investigated.

If challenged by the out of power party, just say,
"Don't you trust your government?"

Rule 10-2
Punch Card voting has holes it!

**Chads a1·e the little bits of paper punched out to mark
the hole next to the voter's choice.**

The punch card voting system (Votomatic-type) has
some holes in it. Every time the cards are fed through the
counter machine, the counter comes up with a different
total. It seems that transporting the punch card ballots from
the precinct to a central location for counting does damage
them. The bending and shaking of the computer cards while
the election clerks put them in their box for transporting and
the taking of the cards out of the box for counting will
cause chads to fall out, making it appear the voter voted for
more candidates in a race than they should have, thus the
ballot will be spoiled and not counted.

Rule 10-3
Gum up the works!

Moist the punch cards. The counting machine will reject moist cards. This will slow up the counting. You may have to examine each punch card one by one. Handling the cards will give you a chance to punch out chads and spoil votes for the other party or candidate.

Rule 10-4
Design a ballot to confuse the voters.

The Butterfly Ballot

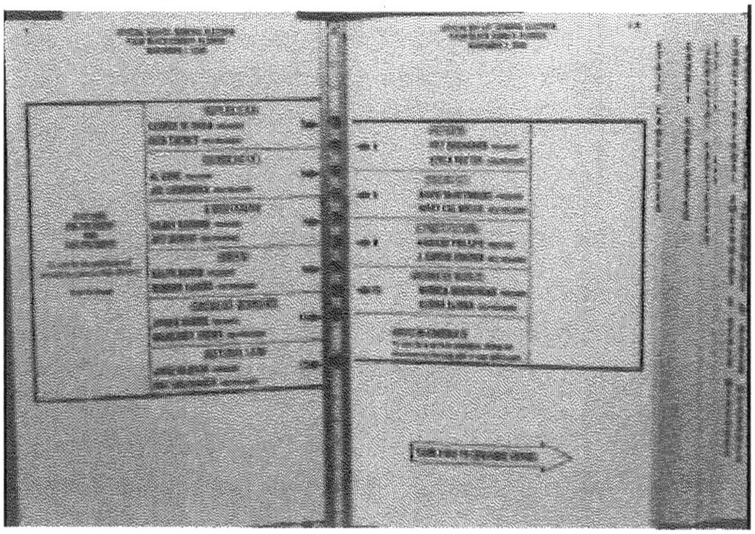

This Palm Beach, Florida ballot was printed in such a way that many people who wanted to vote for Democrat AJ Gore ended up voting for Republican Pat Buchanan.

The design of the ballot would give them a reason for a recount if they found that they were losing! If they were winning, everything is alright!

Remember, you don't have to steal or change every vote to win, just enough to win.

> **George Washington is the only president
> who didn't blame the previous
> administration for·
> his troubles.**
>
> Author Unknown

Chapter **11:**

Recounts

Rule 11-1
Count and recount until you win!

The purpose of a recount is to win the election after you lost the first count! No one demands a recount of a close election to get an honest accounting of their loss. If you don't win the recount, keep counting until you win! Every time you handle the ballots, you have an opportunity to discredit or mark a ballot. If you need twenty votes to win and you can change five ballots each time you have a recount, have five recounts.

The most famous recount is the Bush-Gore Presidential recount in Florida in 2000. The race was determined by the US Supreme Court.

What happened?

In my opinion, the state was called for Gore before the votes were done being counted. Normally, the Democrats hold back a few counties until they know how many votes they need to win the state, but they did not do this because the news media called the state for Gore as the polls closed, based on exit polling.

Later that night, the Democrats realized they did not have enough votes to win, so they demanded a recount. Recount until you win, was the goal! The five counties they wanted to recount were counties they controlled! During the recount, they changed the way they were counting and kept changing the definition of a spoiled ballot. They were trying to throw out enough Bush ballots for Gore to win.

The Supreme Court stepped in and ruled that the laws on recounts would be the same in all the counties. Bush won by a margin of only 537 votes out of almost 6 million cast

     A hanging chad is the price of paper left hanging after the voter punches the hole next to the candidate he is choosing.

Rule 11-2

Discredit enough ballots of your opponent to win.

     If the election is held on paper ballots, mark the

ballot with a piece of pencil under your fingernail or hidden behind a ring so the ballot looks like the voter voted for more than one candidate in the contested race. The ballot will be disqualified and thrown out. They lose a vote.

If the election is held on machines, find a way to challenge the machine or precinct they came from. Both sides will lose vote, but your opponent will lose the most.

If the election is held on computers, as you handle the punch cards, you can bend them or shake them and chads will fall out. This will change the count. It's a risk, you may gain some votes or lose some voles, but at this point, you may have nothing to lose.

Remember, recount until you win!

Rule 11-3
Make the math on your side.

If the math is not on your side, make it so! Reverse the totals in the race between candidates X and Y. You gain voles, they lose voles.

Add wrong. Total up a column of numbers and add a few voles. You gain whatever you can get away with.

Rule 11-4
Find discover votes that were as of yet, uncounted.

If the election is held on paper ballots,
A. Erase votes for your opponent and mark the ballot for your candidate. They lose a vote and you gain a vote.
B. Find uncounted paper ballots in the trunk of the car of a party precinct worker.

"I forgot to turn these in, but they need to be counted and added to our candidate's total."

You gain whatever you can make believable.

If the election is held on voting machines,

A. Find a machine that was never counted. The machine could be found in a friendly precinct polling location or back in the county warehouse. Make sure there are enough votes on the machine for your candidate to win.
B. Find a way of disqualifying precincts or machines that went against you.

If the election is held on computer voting:
A. Have your man reprogram the computer to recount so you win.
B. Disqualify the ballots by either punching new holes in them or filling in the hanging chads with your finger and thumb as you "examine" each one, one at a time.

A newspaper repolter asked the incumbent Senator involved in a recount if he was worried about the election.

The Senator said, "No. I was in the countryside yesterday and had all but given up hope until I passed a man on a mule. He had my bumper sticker on the rump of the mule and a ballot box on the back of his mule. I think that box will be in town by tomorrow afternoon."

Chapter 12:

Dirty Tricks

Like working on election day, the goal is not to turn every vote but to turn just enough to ensure that your party wins. Some so called, "dirty tricks" may not be illegal, but they do, and have continue to have, an impact on the outcome of elections.

Rule 12-1
Use distortion, misrepresentation and false rumors about the opposition.

Two guys went into the bar in the resort part of the state. As they drank their drinks, they started a conversation with the bartender. "Say, this Republican candidate for governor sure is a qualified candidate. Too bad he is dry. You know he is going to try to make the state dry as soon as he gets elected!"

Then they move on to the next tavern.

It does not have to be in a bar. In 1960 in New York City and Chicago, Kennedy workers rode the elevators all day, up and down, in the same skyscrapers. As soon as the doors of the elevators closed, one of them would say something like, "Did you hear what Nixon said? That guy is going to get us into a war!"

All day long they created negative impressions about Nixon for thousands of would-be voters.

It does not have to be true to harm the opposition. Just believable.

Rule 12-2
The October Surprise.

The October Suprise is when the opposition makes a surprise last minute charge hoping that the opposition can't recover or respond before election day.

Candidate Reagon was charged by President Carter's campaign to have made a last-minute deal with the Iranians to hold our Embassy Employees hostage until after the election. It was false, but many Americans believed it and voted for Carter.

Do mailings that arrive on the day before the election charging or exposing your opponent with something the voters will not like. The opposition will not have time to respond!

One candidate sent anonymous letters out attacking himself Knowing when they would be delivered, he pre-scheduled a press conference attacking his opponent for sending out the letters.

All the innocent opponent could do was deny he sent the letters.

In a Midwestern state, the party headquarters sent out a press release saying that they had checked out the rumor that their opponent's campaign for governor was financed partly by drug money from organized crime, but were unable to prove any of it. Never the less, the rumor keeps popping up.

The candidate and the press denounced the tactic as unfair, but gave it more publicity every time they talked about it.

If you tell a lie often enough people will begin to believe it. Even if you lie about your opponent, the truth is slow coming out.

Rule 12-3
Attack the character of your opponent.

Would you vote for a person who had a brother who was a practicing Homosapien? How about if you learned that his sister in New York City was a thespian? What if the candidate himself was accused of matriculating with young women at college or that he emulated older boys at a certain playground in your district? He himself subscribes to a phonographic magazine.

Would you still vote for him if you knew he attempted to interest a group of innocent Boy Scouts in philately?

The smear is perhaps the most widely used political trick. Grover Cleveland was accused of fathering an illegitimate child. Down south, a black woman traveled the state the months before the election telling white voters that she was the daughter of the US Senator running for reelection.

Rule 12-4
Don't let your opponent's voters get to the polls.

New Jersey Governor Chris Christy is accused of causing a traffic problem on a bridge. He is not the first.

In Columbia, South Carolina, Senator Strom Thurmond was running for reelection. The City of Columbia is the State Capital and votes Democratic. Across the river, is the County of Lexington. It votes Republican. Every morning about 100,000 voters drive across two bridges into Columbia to go to work.

On election day, after the Lexington voters had crossed the bridge into Columbia, the Democrat Mayor closed both bridges for repaving. (He later said the bridge work had been scheduled for months. He forgot it was election day.) The closest bridge, north or south, was 52 miles one way, 104 miles round trip. It looked like the Senator was going to lose 100,000 votes.

The Senator's Office phoned the Mayor's Office and told them that if the bridges were not open in one hour, he would have the National Guard, with tanks, open the bridges.

The bridges were opened and the Senator won reelection.

Rule 12-5
Get rid of the other party's campaigners or keep them talking to you so they can't talk to anyone else,

I love it when someone from the other party comes to my door. I can keep them there for an hour talking politics. This way I know they aren't talking to my neighbors.

If you see some campaigners working the neighborhood or shopping mall, tell them you just got a phone call from their headquarters and they want to meet them at a restaurant. Name a restaurant out of the area. They will stop campaigning and drive to the restaurant and wait for an hour for no one to meet them.

Rule 12-6
Use official powers to harass your opponent's people.

Make a list of the cars used by your opponent's leadership team and key campaign workers. Make anonymous calls to the police and report the cars stolen.

The police will stop and retain the cars and anyone found in them for hours.

Rule 12-7
Infiltrate your opponent's inner circle.

Put a mole inside your opponent's organization.
Find out information only the insiders know. Plant
misinformation into their research about your candidate.

Sometimes you can steal or delay shipments of much
needed printed materials. If they are planning a dinner and
have ordered a special pamphlet to hand out, call the printer
and reschedule the delivery or pickup time. Make changes
to the message or design.

Cause confusion. Change or cancel meetings. Send
out memos. Leak information to the press.

Don't get caught.

Rule 12-8
Misinformation on election day.

Challenger Smith was expected to win the election.
Campaigners passed out flyers in front of the polls on
election day to voters as they went into the building to vote.
The flyer said, "Vote for Smith. Pull lever 9."

The problem was, lever 9 belonged to his opponent.

Rule 12-9
Block your opponent's message.

Candidate Smith learned that the night before Election Day, his opponent was going to run a half hour program at 11 p.m. on Channel 8. He was afraid that his
opponent was going to expose him for something he did
several years ago.

Smith bought 5 minutes of ad time at 10:55 on
Cham1el 8. He ran a 60 second commercial for himself; then
he played the National Anthem. Then aired 60 seconds of

blank screen. Viewers though the station had signed off for the night and switched the channel. Few saw Smith's opponent's program!

12-10
Buying Votes.

When I was in my young 20's, I ran as a Democrat for the State House in my southern home state. My opponent in the Democrat Primary was a young man I had gone to high school with, Walter. He was a jock who blew out his knee at the University level and returned to work in his father's gas station. His father was a "Good Old Boy" in the local Party.

My state has something called, "Gas Money." You can give the paster cash to pay for gas so their members can drive to the polls on election day. It's not a bribe. You are not buying votes. It's for gas.

Walter and I did a series of debates in the local dirt poor black churches around town. Before each debate, Walter's father would stand before the church congregation and announce he was giving the pastor gas money for anybody who wanted to vote for his son on election day. He would hold up the cash, all fanned out and make a show of handing it to the pastor.

There were only about 100 to 300 members of these churches. The first church, he gave $800, the next $1000.

The last debate we did, his father made a show of giving the pastor $1500 in gas money.

When the pastor introduced us for the debate it went something like this:

"Tonight, we have the two candidates running in the Democrat primary next week for the State House. I want to introduce to you the greatest thing to happen to Black People since Jesus Christ, Walter (Blank), and his oppo-

nent," (he paused, did not speak for about 30 seconds.
Snapped his fingers about three times like he was trying to
remember my name.) "Can't remember his name. Doesn't
matter!"

Gas Money used right is the next best thing to
legally buying votes!

Of course nothing beats buying votes with
taxpayer's money. Giveaway programs like Social Security,
Food Stamps and Obamacare are good examples of programs once established create a constituency that will
always vote for the party that will maintain or expand their
"FREE STUFF!"

All my life I have heard the Democrats say to the
older voters, "If the Republicans get elected, they will
take away your Social Security!" Can anyone name a
single Republican who has entered a bill to abolish Social
Security?

Rule 12-11
Pad your own pocket.

You have thousands in campaign contributions
coming in. Wouldn't you love to have some of that? Well,
you can!

Charge your campaign royalties for using your
picture! Every time you organization uses your likeness or
name on a bumper sticker or brochure, they pay you a
royalty fee!

Give your campaign a personal loan. Charge the
organization 20 percent interest, compounded daily! Each
year, have the campaign organization pay you only the
interest. You can collect thousands of dollars from your
own campaign organization over the years. It's all legal! I
hope!

> **"Democracy: Where any two idiots can out vote a genius."**
> Unknown

Chapter 13:

Intimidate the Other Party's Workers

Rule 13-1
Use Law Enforcement to intimidate the other party's volunteers.

Democrat Dollars

I am not talking about using the Police to intimidate someone wearing a Bush button or towing away the cars of the other party's clerks on election day. Use the power of government to put the fear of your total control of government, law enforcement and the courts in them! Here is one of the most horrendous examples I have ever heard of in modern times, and I lived it.

In 1970, I was the State Chairman of the South Carolina Teenage Republicans. We had 25,000 dues paying high school age members. We were a larger organization than the adult Republican Party in the state. I lived in Charleston with my parents and was a senior in high school. My older brother, Eddie, was a student at the University of South Carolina and the State Chairman of the Young Americans for Freedom YAF also had about 25,000 college age students.

It was August and for the first time in almost 100 years the Republican Party had a credible candidate running for Governor. For the first time in 100 years, we had a chance to win. The Democrat Governor reacted by calling a special session of the State Legislature that summer. The State Legislature in 1970 was 98 percent Democrat. They met in Special Session for almost 30 days for about a million dollars a day. Back then a million dollars was a lot of money! The Governor said the reason for the special session was that the State's Tercentennial (300th) Birthday was three years away and the legislature had failed to plan for it.

The mostly Democrat special session approved a $32 million TV, radio, and newspaper advertising campaign, to be spent from September 1, to Election Day in November of that year, featuring every Democrat running for state wide office! The ads were to tell the people of South Carolina about the State's Birthday Party in three years, and how much progress has been made, and how great the state is. The bill also created a, "Tricentennial Coin," to be sold to the tourists. The Governor promised that the sale of the coin would raise enough money to repay the state the cost of the advertising campaign.

Eddie and I, and others, saw this as taxpayer sponsored political campaign ads for the Democrats!

About the first week of September, he came up with the idea of creating, "Democrat Dollars!" to spoof the whole taxpayer paid advertising campaign. Democrat Dollars were hand drawn. Printing was done on a hand cranked mimeograph machine on yellow, red and blue paper, never green! They were the size of a dollar bill, but looked nothing like a real dollar bill! We had a, "Nearly 100" dollar bill, "Celebrating almost 100 years of One-Party Rule." We had a, "50 Dollar" bill highlighting the fact that South Carolina is number, "50 in students with college degrees." Our, "$7 bill," said South Carolina is, "Seventh in per capita in state taxes!" Finely, we had a, "$1 bill," celebrating, "One Party Rule!"

It was obvious that this was not real money. Two of the bills said, "Don't let them PLAY with your MONEY!" on the back.

Eddie and I, and members of our two organizations would hand them out as political pamphlets. We would go into department stores and put them into the pockets of the shirts and pants on the racks. We would leave them with our tips and on the tables at restaurants. People were getting a chuckle reading them. No one thought that they were real money. The thought that someone might, never crossed our minds.

I came home from school one day, about the third week of September, and my mother was standing in the kitchen as white as a ghost! She stuttered and said that she had just received a phone call from the FBI. They said that they are going to put you boys in jail!

She said that an Agent Ido had called.

"Ido," I thought. "Sounds like a fake name."

I phoned the Charleston and Columbia FBI offices and asked for Agent Ido. "Nobody here by that name. We do not have an Agent Ido in South Carolina," I was told. So, I got the FBI's Agent's name on the phone and told him I wanted to report a Democrat impersonating an FBI Agent, something that is against the law. I explained to him about the Democrat Dollars. The agent laughed and told me that it sounded like someone was trying to intimidate me. He said that if Agent Ido ever called back to invite him over. The FBI would like to meet him!

The next week, Agent Ido phoned late enough in the afternoon for me to be home from high school to take his call. He said that he was very busy and if he found any more funny money in circulation, he would arrest us!

I told him, believing that he was a fake, that Dick Tracy doesn't phone Scarface and tell him, "Stop kidnapping people or I'll arrest you. If you are real, come and get me!" I taunted him.

He said that he was too busy to arrest us today, but that he would if he found any of our money in circulation.

This only reinforced in my mind that he was a fake!

Each week I got a similar phone call from Agent Ido. The conversation went about the same. He did nothing to make me believe that he was real!

The first week of October, I got a call from the State Chairman of the Republican Party. With a quiver in his voice, he said that I needed to call the U.S. Marshal's Office.

I spoke with the U.S. Marshal, an appointee of President Nixon. **He told me that the Secretary of the South Carolina Democrat Party has filed an Official Complaint with his office charging my brother and I with Counterfeiting U.S. Currency!**

I described the Democrat Dollars to him and told him about the calls from Agent Ido. He laughed and said he had not seen the bills and did not know of any Agent Ido. However, he wanted me to know about the complaint. At the end of the phone conversation he said, "I am so busy that I can't get to you until after the election. You understand?" (There was a, "wink, wink," in his voice!)

We went out and printed 25,000 more sheets of Democrat Dollars!

I received threatening phone calls weekly from Agent Ido, but he kept saying that he was too busy to arrest us.

Election Day came and went. The Democrats retained all state-wide seats. They still controlled 98 percent of the State Legislature. The 100 years of One-Party Rule continued.

Two weeks after the election, on a Friday afternoon, Agent Ido phoned and said that he was, "pissed!" I had been ignoring his threats and had continued to circulate my funny money against his orders! He said he was coming to my house that night at 5 p.m. and arrest us!

Eddie had come home from college for the weekend.

I phoned the FBI and spoke with the agent I had spoken to almost two months earlier. He said that since my last call, he had been doing some research. "The FBI does not have an Agent Ido, but the Secret Service does have an Agent Ido. And that is who you have been pissing off!"

I phoned a Republican lawyer I knew. He said that normally he advises his clients to cooperate, but that it seemed too late for that advice.

5 p.m. came and went. No Agent Ido. 6 p.m. came. No Agent Ido. About 7 p.m., a dark blue car pulled up in front of our house. Two men looking like Joe Friday on the TV show Dragnet waked up to our door. My father answered the door. The man in fount waved a card about chest high and said, "Secret Service. I'm Agent Ido. Out of my way! I'm coming in!"

My dad blocked the door and said, "I want to see some ID!"

"You just did," Ido said, surprised.

"No! You just waved something in front of my face. I could not tell if it was a credit card or a driver's license. I want to see some ID before you come into my house!"

"I have already shown you my ID. Get out of my **way. I'm coming in!"**

"Not until I see some ID!" my father said firmly.

Ido pulled out his ID and handed it to my father. Then my father let them enter the house.

My father worked at the Charleston Naval Base. He was in charge of all the pumps on all the Polaris Submarines in the Atlantic Fleet. He had Top Secret Clearance. He was a veteran of World War II and the Korean War. I have never seen my father afraid until that night!

The Agents said that con-men were passing our money in the rural parts of the State. Poor people were giving change for the $7 bill.

"*All* the better reason to get the Democrats out of

office. They have been in charge of the educational system for the past 100 years in this state, and people still can't tell fake money when they see it." my brother argued.

We argued that the Democrat Dollars were political pamphlets and thus First Amendment protected Free Speech.

Agent Ido said that our, "funny money" too closely resembled U.S. currency.

"Have you seen our, "funny money?" I asked him.

When my brother said, "You have sold your badge to the South Carolina Democrat Patty! Agent Ido knocked him to the floor, rolled him over and handcuffed is hands behind his back.

My dad objected. Ido told him to be silent or he would indite him as a coconspirator in counterfeiting. He could go to Leavenworth Prison for 20 years and lose his federal pension.

Eddie, now sitting on the coffee table with his hands cuffed behind his back, continued to mouth off

Ido told us that he was going to hang Eddie from the pine tree in front of our house as a sign to anyone else who would try to over throw the sovereign government of the United States! He claimed that at the end of the American Civil War the South tried to flood the North with fake Green Backs. Army Officers in the field were given author- ity to try anyone caught with funny money and hang them on the spot. He was claiming that 120-year-old law as his authority in this case.

We said, "We are not trying to overthrow the sovern government of the United States! We are trying to overthrow the sovern government of the State of South Carolina, but by the electoral process!"

That is when I first saw my father afraid, for us, not himself My father said, "OK, let's all just calm down here. Eddie, shut up! What do you want

Ido said that he wanted all the funny money we had left.

I spoke up and said, "Only Eddie knows where it is. If you hang him, you will never find it. You will have to unhandcuff him and we will go and get it."

He unhandcuffed Eddie. We both went back to my bedroom where we had a stack of the sheets or Democrat Dollars hidden between the mattress. Telling him it was all we had left; we gave Ido half or what we had. The election was over. We did not need them all. He was not being truthful with us so we felt we had no obligation to be honest with him!

Ido said that if he found any more funny money in circulation, he would be back with a warrant and fire axes. He said that he'd chop all the sheet rock out of our house looking for it and leave us with thousands of dollars of damage! Then he started to leave...

"Wait!" Eddie said. "You have seized my properly. I want a receipt!"

"What?" Ido said.

"I want a receipt. The United States government has seized my personal property. I want a receipt!"

Ido opened his briefcase and took out the stack of Democrat Dollars and a U.S. Secret Service Receipt form. Ido counted the sheets, filled out the form and signed it and gave my brother a copy.

I reported what happened to the local and state Republican Party leaders. "Welcome to South Carolina politics," is all they said. We never were charged with anything or heard from Agent Ido again.

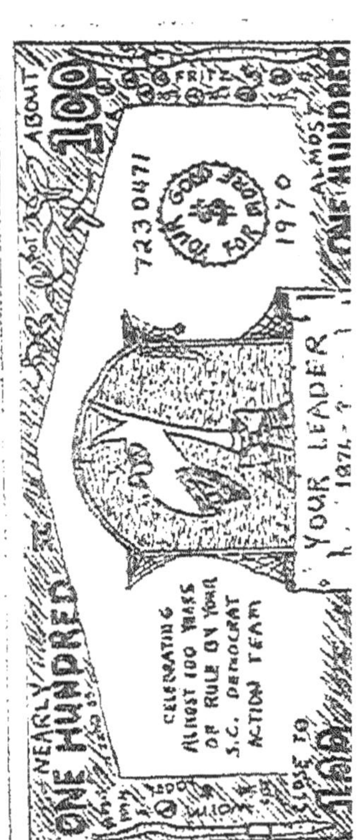

ABOUT 100
FRITZ
ONE HUNDRED
NEARLY
ALMOST
ONE HUNDRED
723 0471
YOUR GOOD FOR NOTHIN
1970
YOUR LEADER 1874 - ?
CELEBRATING ALMOST 100 YEARS OF RULE BY YOUR S.C. DEMOCRAT ACTION TEAM

FRITZ
FIFTY
UNBER STUDENTS COLLEDGE DGREES
YOUR TREASURER

SEVENTH
SEVENTH
IS YOUR MONEY
IN PER CAPITA INCOME GOING FOR STATE TAXES SOUTH CAROLINA RANKS SEVENTH IN THE NATION
1970
723 0471
YOUR GOOD FOR NOTHIN

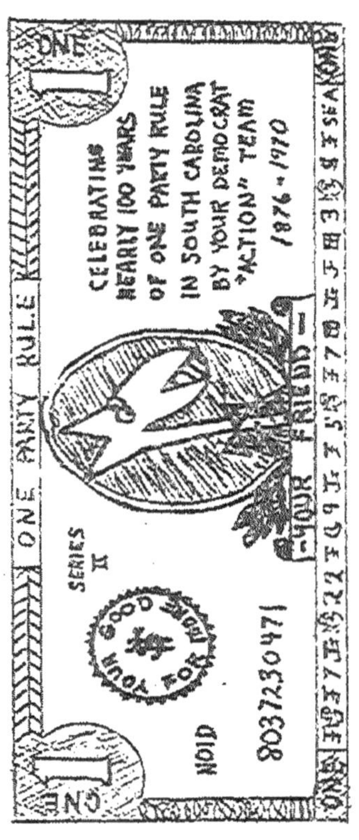

ONE
ONE PARTY RULE
ONE
CELEBRATING NEARLY 100 YEARS OF ONE PARTY RULE IN SOUTH CAROLINA BY YOUR DEMOCRAT "ACTION" TEAM
1876 - 1970
SERIES II
YOUR GOOD FOR NOTHIN
VOID
8037230471
YOUR FRIEND
ONE

100
KEEP THOSE
THAt,1tS ,or .NEARLY
IN HUBERT WE TRUST
THIS NOTE IS AS GOOD AS ANY ACTION TEAM PROMISE
100
100
YEARS OF ONE PARTY RULE

C• ll3 flfWG 106 4l!flll&
a f <>NI PA tl¼ 'l!<Jbi
i:, r,T IJ;T T\IRM
PLA'1 u f 1
MON
50
50
LEROY

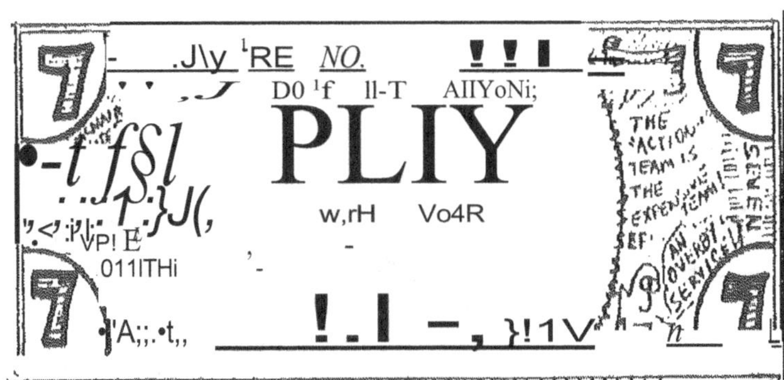
7
J\y RE NO.
!!!
D0 f ll-T AllYoNi;
PLIY
w,rH Vo4R
THE ACTION TEAM IS THE EXPENSIVE
7
7
!.I — , }!1V

1
CELEBRATING 100 YEARS OF ONE PARTY
1
IN HUBERT WE TRUST
ONE
YOU'RE GOOD FOR MORE
WEST
ONE PARTY RULE

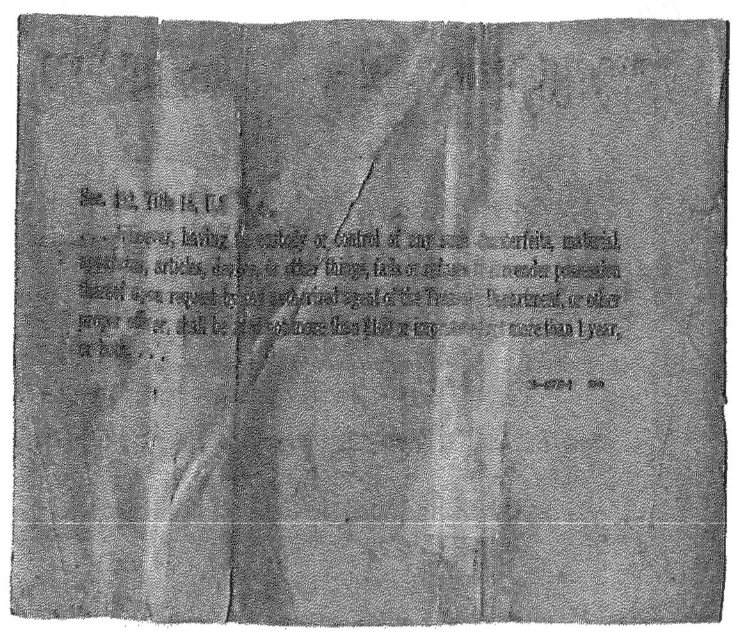

UNITED STATES SECRET SERVICE
TREASURY DEPARTMENT

ORIGINAL

RECEIPT FOR CONTRABAND

Received from _Edward Carl Facell 1857 Monroe ST_

The following described contraband:

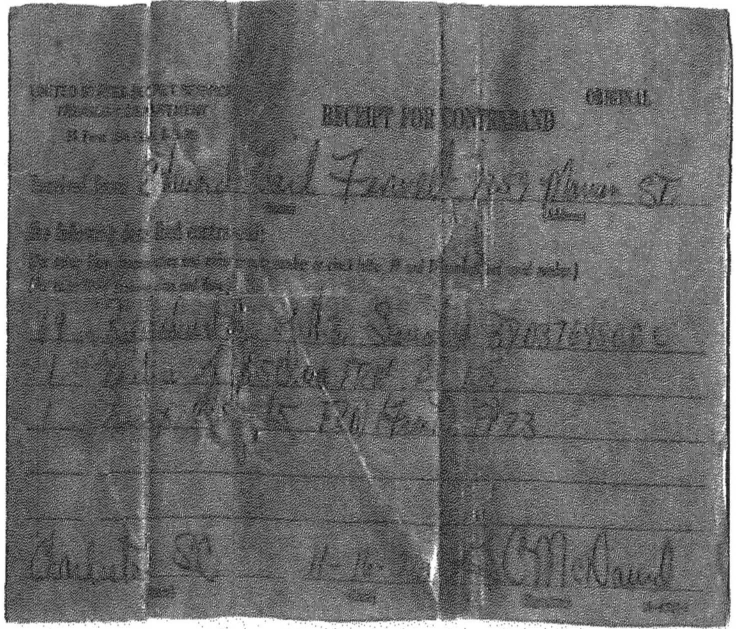

Sec. 142, Title 18, U.S.C.

... whoever, having the custody or control of any such counterfeits, material, apparatus, articles, devices, or other things, fails or refuses to render possession thereof upon request by any authorized agent of the Treasury Department, or other proper officer, shall be fined not more than $100 or imprisoned not more than 1 year, or both . . .

3rd Ward Fennell

I ran for City Council against a longtime incumbent. I wanted to represent the 3rd Ward, so I used the nickname, "3rd Ward Fennell." About five weeks before the election I received a letter from the County Clerk saying that she had gotten one anonymous phone call saying that perhaps, maybe, there was a chance, someone might be confused into thinking that I was the incumbent if I called myself; "3rd Ward Fennell." I was there for forbidden to use it and if I continued to use it, she would prosecute me to the fullest extent of the law!

I wrote her back saying that I was sorry, "I did not intend to imply or confuse anyone into thinking I was the incumbent. I would not want the lady's record!" I told her that I had tried my political nickname on my friends before deciding to use it and no one said maybe, perhaps someone would be confused into thinking I was the incumbent.

If she prosecutes me, I wrote her, then she also would have to prosecute people like Indiana Jones and Nevada Smith, "because someone might think they were the incumbent office holders in their states."

I offered to buy a rubber stamp saying, "I am not the incumbent! I would not like the lady's record!" and stamp it on all my literature under the phrase," 3rd Ward Fennell.

"If that did not satisfy you, please prosecute me. I need the publicity," I wrote her.

Two weeks later, I was at a Republican County Executive Committee and the County Prosecutor walked up to me and asked what I had been up to.

I told him I was running for City Council in my community.

Well, he told me the County Clerk had approached him asking for a Grand Jury investigation of my life! My entire life!!! He said that he told her that he did not have the budget to investigate me for a political nickname. He had drug lords and organized crime to investigate!

The last three weeks before the election, she held a press conference, one a week, calling me, "The Outlaw Candidate!" "The Criminal Candidate!" and "A Radical!"

The city government phoned me once a week to tell me that my yard signs were either one square inch too large or one inch too close to the curb somewhere. In each case, they said that they would have to pick up the signs because they were illegal!

I told them that if they touched my signs, legally in a supporter's yard, they would trigger a U.S. Justice Department Investigation!

They left the signs alone.

We had a 4 percent voter turnout and I lost the election. If I had had a bigger family I would have won!

Six weeks later, she resigned from office and moved to Chicago for a job. The sitting members of the Council appointed someone else to fill her seat.

Rule 13-2
Remembe1; you are in charge!

Today the laws and tax codes are so complicated and complex that almost everybody is in "noncompliance" to something! The Federal Register alone is over 79,000 pages. If someone challenges you, ask them if they really want the government rooting around their business practices or looking into their taxes!

They will back down!

> **"Politicians and diapers have one thing in common -   they both should be changed regularly and for the same reason!"**
>
> Unknown

The Election Manipulator's Manual's Election Deception Award

**Awarded to the candidate with the most
deceptive election tactics
that resulted in the election of someone who
otherwise might not have won the election.**

(Since this is the first award, I have reviewed elections in my
lifetime for consideration. Starling with the 2014 election, I
am inviting the readers of this book to nominate campaigns
and candidates for consideration.)

......and the winner is:

Congressman Mendel J Davis
(D) S.C.

Campaigns of 1971   1972

When Congressman Mendel Rivers D-SC (1941-
1970) died in office, his son Mendel Rivers Jr. was one year
too young to nm for his father's office. Mendel Davis was a
staffer in the Congressman's office. He was also River's

godson.

Mendel Davis ran for office in a special election, almost never mentioning his last name. *"Return Mendel to Congress!"* was his mantra.

For his reelection campaign in 1972, his campaign slogan was, *"Return Mendel to Washington, 33 years **working for you!"***

Being in his early 20's, he dodged the question during the campaign. On election night, at his victory party, finally a TV reporter questioned him about being in his 20's yet claiming 33 years working for this district!?

His reply was that he had taken his 18 months in Congress and Rivers' 31 years in Congress and together someone named "Mendel" had represented this district for 33 years.

For that, we are giving him the first The Election Deception Award!

Nominate your candidate for The Election Deception Award. The winner will be announced in undated The Election Manipulator's Manuals.

The person who nominates the winner will win a copy of The Election Manipulator's Manual.

Send your nomination and a narrative of what the deception was about and how it impacted the election to;

The Election Manipulator's Manual
Jerry@28thStreet.Biz

Dictionary
of Election Words and Tenns

Ballot - List of candidates from which the voter has to choose from.

Ballot Box - Aller the voter marks his choices on his ballot, the ballot is dropped into this locked box for counting after all the ballots have been cast.

Challenged Ballot - When a voter cannot prove who he is or that he lives in the precinct, but wants to vote in this precinct, he is allowed to vote on a paper challenged ballot. The ballot is placed in an envelope and sealed. The words, "Challenged Ballot," are written on the envelope. There is a hearing after the election to determine if the envelope is to be opened and the ballot counted.

Challenged Voter - A person who presents himself to the Clerk in order to get a ballot for voting. The Clerk or Watcher did not believe the person was qualified to vote, thus the voter was challenged.

Clerk (Poll) - Official worker in the Precinct Poll on Election Day. Is supposed to be neutral, but usually is an active party member.

Election Chairman or Judge - Person in charge of proceedings at the polls on Election Day. Appointed by the local government.

Fast Count - Ballots are counted quickly by poll workers working together as a team to manipulate the outcome, too fast for watchers or the public to keep up with what they are doing.

Floater Voter - Fake voter, not the person whom they are pretending to be on election day. Person who floats from one precinct to another on election day and votes illegally several times.

Full Slate Law - The Full Slate Law states that if the voter does not vote for a certain number of candidates, then their vote will not be counted. Example: A county has seven representatives in the State House. The Full Slate Law says that a voter must vote for seven candidates or his or her vote will not be counted. If the opposition party only fields five candidates, then a supporter has to vote for at least two members of the other patty for their vote to count. The voter is forced to vote for someone they do not support. The U.S. Supreme Court has ruled this unconstitutional.

Hanging Chad - The piece of paper left hanging after the voter punches the hole next to the candidate he is chosen. See page 75 for photo.

Master Switch or Lever - On a voting machine there is a lever that can be thrown that will register a vote for every candidate for that one party. Punch Card Computer voting has a similar hole that can be punched.

Nonpartisan Election - An election that does not allow party affiliation. Mostly local elections.

Papper Ballot: A list of candidates running for office printed on paper. Voter's mark who they want for office and put the paper ballot in the Ballot Box for counting after the election is over.

Poll Challenger - A Poll Watcher that has the authority to challenge a voter.

Poll Watcher - Represents a candidate or party, and is not an Election Official. He has no legal right to address voters directly. Must bring all inquiries to the Precinct Chairmen.

Polling Place - Building housing voting machines used on Election Day.

Precinct Chairman Election Judge - In charge of the polling place on Election Day.

Provisional Ballot - See Challenged Ballot.

Slow Count - Ballots are counted taking a longer than needed time to count. The poll officials are waiting for the opponent's precincts to report so that they will know how many votes they will have to report for their candidate or party to make up the difference to insure victory.

Spoiling a ballot - The act of tampering with a ballot so it will be disqualified and not counted.

Straight **Party (Voting)** - When a voter votes for every member of one party.

String Voting - String voting can be used on paper ballots or machine voting. The voter is given a string with knots in it. When laid out on the ballot or machine face, where the knot is the voter is instructed to vote for that candidate. This is legal, unless the voter is being paid with money or liquor or had been intimidated.

Ticket Splitter - A voter who splits his ballot between the different party's candidates.

Voting the Books - Illegally voting for someone on the registration books that has not voted.

Why pay money to have your family tree traced; go into politics and your opponents will do it for you.

-Author Unknown

Send your

Election Stories

and nominations for

The Election Deception
Award

to

Jerry@28thStreet.Biz